The Smell of Diesel

A personal account of the working life of a lorry driver from the 1960's onwards

D1513057

David John Whitfield

A CIP catalogue record for this book
is available from the British Library.

ISBN: 978 1 507577 25 7

Book cover courtesy of
NA3T Archive of Transport Travel and Trade

Typesetting and Formatting:
Beaten Track Publishing,
Burscough, Lancashire.
www.beatentrackpublishing.com

ACKNOWLEDGEMENTS

GRATEFUL THANKS TO:

WILLIAM WRIGHT
GYLES CARPENTER
BILL REID
JIM McLAREN
NA3T ARCHIVE OF TRANSPORT TRAVEL AND
TRADE
GRAHAM ROBERTSON
SLUDGE G

TABLE OF CONTENTS

CHAPTER ONE
EARLY WORKING LIFE

The seeds were sown in the 1950s, when trying not to fail at grammar school I used to walk home from school via the lorry park in Avenham Preston. The lorry park was very large, and it needed to be as Preston was on the main A6 north -south trunk route to and from Scotland. As I usually arrived there around 4-15 pm it was possible, with patience, to see dozens of lorries enter the park within the next hour. At the time, my favourite haulage contractor was Robsons Border Transport and to see the Fodens, all with their different border name was a lovely sight.

Leaving the lorry park and walking the longer way home, I could go past a company that had Thames Trader 6D artics with the new four-inline trailers, a bit closer to home another company had Bedford and Austin rigid lorries. During school holidays was the best, plenty of free time during the week meant I could cycle to many places in the area and one of my favourite spots was a nearby bakery. Walter Southworth delivered flour to the bakery with their wagon and drags, and watching the trailers being nosed into the loading bay was, to me anyway, a fantastic sight. Another favourite place to visit was the docks and even though I could not get onto the docks, there was plenty to see from the wrong side of the gates. Sometimes I would cycle down to the riverside to watch the ships passing to and from the docks. There was always somewhere to go and I was never bored as I had an interest in lorries and ships, so I was in a great area to enjoy it all.

It was now 1961, the grammar school and I had parted company earlier than expected, I was still only fifteen, but I had a plan. One of my other interests was animals and farming, and for the last twelve months had been working part- time on a farm near Preston. On leaving school, the farmer took me on full- time, with a wage of three pounds a week. It meant living at the farm, but as I was an independent lad, it didn't bother me leaving home at fifteen. My home and family life was good, but it was my choice and I felt confident about my future. However, it was only twelve months later when the doubts started to set in mainly because of the way the farmer treated me coupled with the workload. The milking of forty odd Ayrshire cows was not a problem when I was part time but twice a day for six days and once on Sundays which was my half day off was proving too much. All the calves had to be cared for, thousands of battery hens to look after, yards to clean and multitude of other jobs. The farmer got me up at 6am then went back to bed. I went for the cows from the fields to start milking on my own and he strolled into the small milking parlour at around 8am. Many times he was off out all day leaving me to try to get through everything on my own. If things went wrong during the day, he blamed me on his return. Some things he should have taught me so that the many problems would not have arisen. If the calves where scouring or a cow had mastitis, I was at fault and even at my young age, I was not prepared to put up with this treatment. After a while, a job was advertised for a drivers mate in a nearby village so after ringing up, I went along for an interview. Arriving in the village and after asking for directions, I found myself walking down a track towards a house next to a very large modern barn type building with wooden cabins down one side. Inside the barn was a mountain of wood shavings, mostly white, but with layers of red and brown here and there. I knocked on the house door and the boss asked me inside, where he began by telling me about his business as sawdust and shavings merchant, he then asked me a couple of questions before showing me around outside. He explained his lorries collected sawdust and shavings from the Lancashire area and delivered them to local farms. In the summer, the white shavings went to a chipboard factory at Annan near Dumfries to be made into chipboards. We had another little chat and to my delight, he offered me the job. I was to start the following Monday with a wage of five pounds plus overtime, which was a lot more than the farm. We both shook hands and I left feeling pleased.

Leaving the farm, I caught the bus to Preston to break the news to Mum and Dad, which was going to be difficult. Whilst working on the farm another family member had been born, I had another brother. On reaching home and after telling my story, Mum said that I would have to sleep down-stairs, as the house was rather full. As well as Mum, Dad and my new brother there was also Pauline, Joan and Andrew my other brothers and sisters. Pleased that it all seemed to be working out and not bothered about my sleeping arrangements, I set off back to the farm to tell the farmer the bad news. He was not pleased at all, arguing that he had put lot of time into training me, which was an absolute lie. The next week was not very pleasant, but by keeping my head down the week soon went.

After a good weekend at home, it was time to start my new job, which meant catching two buses to

Woodplumpton just north of Preston. At 7 20 am on Monday I got off the bus and made the short walk to the yard, following two other lads down the track. One of the lads muttered to his mate "another new one" but said nothing to me. The two lads entered one of the big cabins and I followed a bit apprehensively into the gloomy cabin. Standing around a cast stove were two older men and a tall younger man, all of whom gave the two lads and me a muted greeting. Two more men arrived a couple of minutes later and the older men had just started to chat when the boss Mr. Park strode in, after warming his backside on the stove gave two of the men some instructions and told the men to take two lads with them. Whilst wondering which lorry I was to go out on Mr. Park looked at me and said "Baling today" and not really knowing what he was on about I followed everyone out into the barn.

Down one side of the barn was a large loft about eight feet high and under this was a small rail track with two steel trucks on the rails. Attached to the loft roof in the centre of the track was what looked like a screw press? One of the older men started up an old Nuffield tractor that had a front loader attached and proceeded to dig into the mountain of shavings depositing them on the loft floor. A lad went up onto the loft and I followed Mr. Park and two others underneath to the trucks. Telling me to take notice, I watched as they made a bale of shavings. The steel door on the truck was opened and four rough wooden laths placed lengthways in the bottom and then covered with thick brown paper before the door was closed. When the truck was pushed under an opening in the loft, the lad upstairs filled the truck with shavings, and once full, four more laths and another sheet of paper placed on top. The full truck was pushed under the press and two wires threaded through channels at the bottom of the truck before the press was started. After the press started, it began to compact the shavings, which after reaching its limit stopped itself. The two wires were threaded over the top of the bale again using channels in the press and tightened with pliers, the press was lifted, the door opened and hey presto, a perfect bale of wood shavings. The other truck had been prepared and changed places to go under the press, and so it went on.

As we started, baling two of the lorries were leaving the yard, one being an Austin artic with a Scammell coupling and the other an old Morris FFK flat bed .The remaining lorry left in the yard was an S type Bedford 2 axle rigid that seemed to be in good condition. However my job for the time being was making bales and by baggin time (brew time) I looked like a snowman with dust up my nose and in my hair. Baggin came at 10am and then we all trooped into the cabin, someone had already put the kettle on the stove so everyone started to brew up. One of the older men called Ernie saw that I had no cup never mind tea and sugar thrust a cup at me and said "tea and sugar in me bag." The bag turned out to be a large strawberry basket that Ernie was using to carry his food and brewing stuff. After helping myself, I sat on a spare box, watched, and listened to the others.

Apart from Ernie there was a man called Tom, Paul a man of about 20, and a lad called Dennis. Paul I liked right away as he was a comedian, he soon had everyone, including myself, laughing as he took the Mickey out of the older men, and Tom called him a cheeky young pup. By the end of baggin, I was feeling a lot better, the disappointment of not going out on the road was passing. The morning went quickly and at dinnertime we all headed back to the cabin. Towards the end of dinner, Mr.

Park told Paul to go to Baines for a load. As he looked around his eyes fell on me and to my delight he rasped, "Go with Paul", we were only going to Preston but it was enough for me.

Paul's lorry was the S type Bedford and as I watched Paul changing gears, it prompted me to ask the purpose of the button on the gear stick. Paul explained it was for the 2-speed axle and my immediate thought was to compare it to a three speed on a bike. Paul seemed to know many people as he was always waving to other drivers. On arriving at the mill, Paul reversed into the yard and parked alongside a building that had a large opening in its wall. He explained that I was to go inside and throw the bags of shavings out of the opening and he would build up the load. I jumped on the lorry, and dived through hole to see what appeared to be a snowman. It turned out to be the man who filled the bags by fastening them to a large pipe on the wall. Throwing the first few bags seemed easy as they were light, but every so often a heavy bag came that had more sawdust in it. Gradually the stacks where diminishing but by now Paul was high up on the load and reaching down to grab them off me. We reached the end and I went outside where Paul gave me some ropes and asked me to climb on top of the load and lay them out. He explained he wanted them side to side down the load with two more from front to back. Roping done, we walked round to the office for a ticket, which was given to Paul by a young girl about my age, I decided there and then that I was in love!

Back on the road, we were to deliver the load to a farm near Blackpool and I settled down to enjoy the ride after the exertion of loading. It seemed to me that the lorry was swaying a lot but Paul was very unconcerned, even when he saw me bracing myself on bends in the road. Arriving at the farm, we unloaded the shavings into a barn and Paul wrote a ticket for the farmer who paid us by cheque. It was dark by the time we arrived back at the yard and as it was going home time, I proceeded to empty my boots of shavings and tidy myself up. Paul, who had a van, asked if we wanted a lift to the bus stop, we gladly accepted and along with John and Dennis, we set off for home.

At home, mum told me to get changed, I thought I was quite clean, but in the bathroom, everything I took off showered the room with dust and shavings. After tidying up in a fashion, I went down for my tea, which I had on my own as everyone else had eaten. Suddenly there was a shout from upstairs and my sister dashed down to tell Mum that the bathroom was full of sawdust, what followed was the first of many rebukes about the sawdust in the house.

The weeks and months flew past and I gradually got to know my way around Lancashire and parts of North Wales. Usually I went out with Paul in the Bedford or the Austin artic but occasionally went with old Tom who was a good driver but did not like changing gears. He would struggle up the hills, with the engine on its last breath, and always say at the top of the hill that the engine was useless. Paul used to let me drive the Bedford on farm tracks and I had many lesson from Paul over the months.

When returning to the yard at dinnertimes we would stop at the bakers shop and buy pies and cakes. The two girls serving knew Paul well from his visits and he always sounded the horn when passing the shop. He joked with them in the shop and gradually I was becoming to like girls even more as I gained confidence. I was happy at work especially in Paul's company and the other lads had become good mates, the only one I felt wary of was Ernie.

By this time, I had a motorbike, an Ariel Arrow Sports and whilst only being a learner I felt reasonably safe on it. However, one night when riding home a car came out of a side road right in front of me, the bike hit the side of the car and I flew over the car landing on my hands and knees. My head hit the road and the crash helmet undoubtedly worked perfectly. An ambulance came and took me to the hospital where the doctor examined me before letting me go home, I left the hospital with a gift of sawdust and shavings on the A&E floor. The next morning it was back to the buses to get to work, but was not really bothered as I had put in for my driving test and felt that after all Paul's and my Dad's lessons I would pass easily. A few weeks later I passed the test and Dad and I went down to Bradshaw's garage in Preston where I bought with Dad a Ford Thames 5cwt van that I had set my heart on. It suited me and for a bit of petrol money I collected the lads in a morning and took them home at night. It knocked a good forty five minutes off all our travelling time every day and benefited us all.

The only lorry Mr. Park said I could drive was the S type Bedford and as Paul was now driving the Austin artic, the Bedford was spare. Gradually I was getting more experience and loading and delivering at most of the places that I been too with Paul. Overall, I was beginning to feel more grown up and loved driving the Bedford. The weight of the Bedford was just under the three ton limit, so I was okay to drive it.

Apart from the driving, we all had to work in the yard making bales to fulfil orders. Mr. Park would let us know how many to make and we all got on with it, usually with the boss present, until he would get fed up and head into the house. That was the signal to switch Radio Caroline on and a bit of larking around. Tom and Ernie hated pop music but they were out-voted by the younger ones. When the boss decided to show himself again he would sneak up on us and make us turn the music off. Mr. Park was a decent boss but he sometimes had a foul temper, the first stage of which was to lift his cap to one side of his head, the second and more serious was to throw the cap on the ground. When this happened, it was best to keep your head down and work. Some days he was in a good mood and it was on one of these days he had his accident. We had been baling for an hour or so and Mr. Park was doing the hardest job as usual pressing the up and down buttons for the press. A truck was pushed under the press to make another bale and the boss pressed the down button. He was humming away to himself and never realized that his hand was resting on the top edge of the truck. As the press reached his fingers, he let out an awful noise and fortunately for him he had the presence of mind to reach for the stop button with his other hand. Tom pressed the up button and Mr. Park retrieved his fingers, which were bleeding but not really crushed. He staggered into the house and we did not see him again until late afternoon, Radio Caroline had a few more listeners that day. At baggin time, Paul had us all in stitches as he gave us a rendition of the accident. Holding his hand out, and humming a tune, he then howled falling on the floor holding his hand. Good job the boss did not sneak back out of the house and catch us being so un- sympathetic.

The spring of 1964 was upon us and I was feeling very excited, I was to take the Bedford with a load of shavings to the chipboard factory at Annan. Mr. Park said I was to follow Paul who was driving the Austin artic not just to show me the way but tell me what to do at the factory. We left the yard at five the next morning and joined the A6 northbound at Broughton north of Preston. The M6 was not due to open from Preston to Lancaster until early 1965 so it was the A6 all the way to Carlisle. By the time, we had reached Kendal I was feeling great but going over the right turn bridge in the town I really thought the load was going to fall off, my hands were sweating and as the lorry became level, I was not feeling happy. However by the time we reached the Jungle Café at Shap nothing was bothering me .The café lorry park was full of lorries belonging too many of the famous Scottish, English and Welsh haulage contractors. The Scottish trucks were to me anyway the best and I regarded the drivers as heroes. Although I was only driving a small lorry I felt ten foot tall as Paul and I entered the café. I had been in many transport cafes before but this was the famous one at Shap. The inside of the café was alive with the sound of real lorry drivers and the smell of eggs and bacon was heaven. Paul had been in the café many times before and soon spotted someone he knew, it was a driver from Thorntons from Brock and he was also on his way to Annan with a load of shavings.

After a very large breakfast, we departed the café to continue on towards Penrith and Carlisle. Over the next few miles, Paul pulled ahead and I was glad to see him in front pulling off a lay-by just before Penrith. It was great to see all the lorries coming towards me all sheeted and roped very professionally. Many were hauling steel and I even saw one with anchor chains piled on the trailer. Entering Carlisle, which was very busy I managed to keep Paul insight but generally was enjoying the new sights. Continuing north on the A74 we turned off towards Annan at Gretna, we were nearly there. The factory was just this side of Annan and I turned in behind Paul to wait my turn onto the weighbridge. Whilst waiting I watched a Caledonian driver roping his load and thought it a very craftsman like job. I weighed and followed Paul around to where we had to unload. Unloading meant emptying all the bags onto a huge pile of shavings as we had to take the bags back with us. We did Paul's load first, then mine, finally bagging the empties up. After a cup of tea in the canteen we set off for home where we arrived by mid-afternoon only to be brought back down to earth when told to do some baling. Baling or not, I had really enjoyed the day and could not wait for the next trip to Scotland.

Paul had been courting for a while and as is the way, his girlfriend was pregnant and he was getting married. The worst news he had to tell me was that he was leaving his job to work in Preston. After he left things were never the same and after a row with the boss, I decided to leave myself. Not wanting to be out of work, I faced the situation and went as a driver's mate/ driver for Bridges Transport, a parcel carrier in Preston. I hated it from day one and felt I was slipping backwards on my career. After a few months, I left and went to work for Fred Bamber who was an animal feed manufacturer in Preston. Bamber's had a large mill on St. Georges road in the town and had a good fleet of vehicles including Fodens and Albions. I was to drive a Thames Trader 4D delivering bagged cattle food to farms in Lancashire. The work was heavy and dusty but at least I was driving and on my own. The loads were about six tons and if we did three loads a day it was a bit more money. Delivering was usually not too bad but occasionally some farmer would want his hen food stacked in a cabin that was in the middle of a field with no access to the lorry. After about three months, the boss asked if I wanted to work out of another mill at Halton near Lancaster, the plan being to load at Preston and deliver to the Halton mill. Once unloaded at Halton they would re-load me with farm drops for the Kirby

Lonsdale area. Twice a week or so I was to load limestone flour at a Carnforth quarry and then return to Preston. This suited me right down to the ground, as I was very nearly my own boss and loved the area around Kirby Lonsdale.

By now, I was courting myself with a girl called Margaret and it was going very well. We met two or three times a week and usually went for a drink or to the pictures. I had met Margaret's mum and dad a few times and they seemed alright to me. It was in late 1965 that things got complicated, Margaret was pregnant and it was up to me to tell Margaret's parents the news. Her Dad went mad and shouted, "If this is modern living you can stuff it", not the best choice of words but nothing could be changed now. Even though my Dad said I didn't need to, Margaret and I were to get married. The usual meeting of parents took place, which went badly. Margaret was a Protestant and I a Catholic, which did not go down well with my potential in-laws. In all sincerity they thought Catholics drank too much and somehow inferior to Protestants. However, we got married and for the next few months, I lived with Margaret's parents and endured it for Margaret's sake. In early 1966, my Dad gave us the deposit for a new house even though he was really short of money himself. The house was a new build terraced property in Bamber Bridge south of Preston. It cost £1950 and we moved in in time for the birth of a little girl who we named Sally. I continued working at Fred Bambers for the next twelve months, still doing the Kirby Lonsdale deliveries, it was hard work but until I was twenty one there was else nothing I could do. In July 1967, I was twenty one at last, but with more responsibilities, I needed more money, and then I heard that a local haulage contractor, Ken Ditchfield, wanted drivers. I rang Mr. Ditchfield and he asked me to come up to his yard, which was down a lane at the top of Bamber Bridge. I walked up to Ditchfield's yard as I had no car at the time and entered the garage. Down the left side was a small office and through the window I could see a man sat behind a desk, with a wave he beckoned me to enter before standing up to greet me. Introducing himself as Ken Ditchfield, he asked me to sit down. Mr. Ditchfield was a big man with quite a jovial face and as I sat down, he reached over to shake hands, which I thought was a good start. He began by asking me what I had done in the past, and then where I was working now. He seemed satisfied with my experience and then proceeded to tell me about the job he had vacant.

If I was successful, the lorry I would be driving would be a Dodge K series 2 axle flatbed. His work was mainly off Preston Docks as a sub-contractor for Ulster Ferry and Northern Ireland Trailers. Some other work was with Leyland Rubber and a few other small contracts. The fleet consisted of 2 Dodge K series; an LAD cabbed three axles Dodge and a three axle TK Bedford. There was also an old Leyland Beaver 4x2 tractor unit, which was inside the garage. Without me asking Mr. Ditchfield told me I could earn over eighteen pounds a week, which was six pounds, more than Bambers. He then told me the job was mine and that I could start as soon as possible.

Accepting the job, I said I would have to work my notice, which he agreed to. Thanking him, I left the office on cloud nine practically running home to tell Margaret the news and she was as pleased as I was.

On the following Saturday after working my notice Ken rang me up and asked me to collect a container from the docks on Sunday morning as was the usual weekend practice. The next morning I walked to the yard where another of Ken's drivers who was also going to the docks met me. He gave me the keys for my Dodge and said to follow him, and when we got down to the docks he would put me right. Sitting in a strange vehicle is a bit confusing but I had no problems with anything really.

We arrived at the docks and I followed the other driver into Northern Ireland Trailers office compound. I didn't know it at the time but it was the beginning of an association with the docks and N.I.T. We both got our notes and drove over the road to the crane compound where one of the workers checked our notes before telling the other driver to pull under the crane. Within five minutes, he was loaded and it was my turn. The other driver told me to load the container a bit to the offside but it landed on the nearside and not wishing to be awkward I said nothing and the container was un-shackled. The container was loaded with hanging sides of beef and felt quite heavy, I soon wished the container was more to the offside and felt as though the lorry was leaning too much. On arriving back at the yard the other driver said it would be alright but to take it easy.

The meat was for delivery on Monday at Manchester meat market. I had to be there by 5-30am, so on the Monday morning I set off at 4-15am and after one or two wrong turns arrived at the market. I made my way round the stands until the correct one appeared. A man in white overalls came up to the cab and looked at my notes before telling me to reverse onto a large open door. After getting parked, I went around the back of my lorry where the man was taking the seal off the container doors. He jumped down and told me to open the doors and on doing this, a cloud of white fog hit me in the face, it was from the dry ice used to cool the container.

The meat porter asked me if I wanted a coat and not realising what he meant I said no, as I stood there he said "when you're ready" and then the penny dropped, I was to pass the meat to him. Having refused the coat I put my arms around the first quarter of beef and all became clear as to why the coat was needed. It was a struggle to get the meat to come off the hook as the rope holding the meat to the hook kept bending the wrong way. However, I managed with a lot of exertion, some being easier than others. The hooks were supposed to move in the tracks on the ceiling of the container but no amount of pulling could make them move, so I carried them all to the back. The last one came and boy was I glad, as apart from the exercise my clothes were greasy and smelly. The porter came out with my signed notes and handed me a parcel saying that it was some dinner for me. Once in the cab I looked in the parcel and saw it contained some very thick steaks. Thinking about that night's tea made me feel very hungry so I had some breakfast before ringing Ken. He told me to get the empty container off at N.I.T. and then go to Ulster Ferry further down the docks. At U.F.T., they loaded me with a Lancashire flat for H.J HEINZ at Kitt Green. The load was from Erin Foods in Ireland and even though it was quite high, there was not much weight. On arriving at Heinz, which looked a very busy factory, I checked in and was told they would give me a call when it was my turn. By this time, it was dinner break and a driver I had been talking to said he would show me where the canteen was. The dinner proved to be excellent and not too expensive and I was feeling that no way could I eat steak that night. On arriving back at the lorry park I waited for another hour or so until I was told to pull onto the weigh-bridge ,this done I drove around the factory to get to the loading bays and a checker told me to reverse into an empty bay. Getting the ropes and sheets off proved very difficult as the ropes and sheet ties were all knotted together, but I persevered and the fork truck driver had the load off in no time. In the loading bays were about a dozen artics all loading full pallets of Heinz canned foods.

By now, it was around 3pm and after ringing in again, Ken told me to go back to U.F.T., get the empty flat off and load another one for Kitt Green. All this took the rest of the day and I arrived back at the yard in time to meet some of Ken's other drivers. I found out that a driver the same age as me had started that day and he was driving the TK Bedford. There was Jimmy who drove the other Dodge K series and a huge older man who drove anything and did work in the garage. He was called Eric and I found out later his nickname was Lurch because of his massive size. Leaving for home, I felt tired but well satisfied with my day.

The next day I delivered the load to Heinz and did another one in the afternoon but was too late to go to the docks and re-load. Over the next couple of months, I became very friendly with Alan who started with me, on many days we were running together which made for an enjoyable experience. We both agreed that the job was not really what we wanted and resolved to get jobs with a bigger company. One day Alan and I were told to report to a new company on the docks called Seawheel, all they had was a porta-cabin at the top of the docks and that was it. We entered the cabin and a man about our age greeted us and asked us if we would like a coffee, which I thought was very friendly. Whilst drinking our coffee's he told us we were to get an empty container each at Walter Southworth's yard just outside Rufford .We then had to load in East Manchester at a factory that made garden machinery. It all seemed straightforward, so we set off for Rufford to get the containers. Arriving at Southworths a very friendly man put a container on each of our lorries with a very ancient mobile crane that despite its age did the job very well.

Leaving Rufford we drove across to Chorley and then on the A6 to Manchester. The factory in Gorton proved difficult to find but after asking for directions a couple of times, we arrived before dinner. We found a pie shop as we were hungry, pies and cakes bought we sat in Alan's cab and chatted about the job. We did get round to talking about companies on the docks but had no real plans just yet. After dinner we finished Alan's load and then got stuck into loading me, which took about 2 hours or so. We knew that the containers where going back to the docks so we set off to try to get them unloaded that day. On arriving at Seawheel, we were told that, as Seawheel had no facilities to unload, the dock cranes would lift them of at the required berth and put them on the quayside. It took quite a while to organize this and Alan and I were worried it wasn't going to happen that day which would not please Ken at all. However, it was managed in the late afternoon and after ringing Ken, we were told to return to the yard.

The driver called Jimmy lived at the top of the lane which passed fields before the yard was reached. He was quite a character but didn't like walking down the unlit lane in the dark. Sometimes he would wait at the top of the lane until one of us appeared and then act as though it was pure chance that we had met. If he had to go down the lane on his own he would run like a scared rabbit, unlock the small garage door, fumble for the light and then he was ok. Early one dark morning, Eric the very large driver, got to the garage first and waited for Jimmy. Sure enough, Eric heard the footsteps of the four minute miler approaching and readied himself. Jimmy unlocked the door and reached out for the light switch only to find it covered by one of Eric's spade like hands. Eric had concealed himself at the office corner and only his arm was showing but as it was pitch black Jimmy could see nothing. His shriek must have been heard over most of the Brig and Jimmy wasn't at all happy with Eric.

I continued to work for the dock companies and gradually got to know the depot staff and some of the drivers, which made life a lot easier. There is nothing worse than being ignored and treated as a stranger. We were still loading rubber for Leyland Tyre and Rubber from Liverpool, but it wasn't a job any of us liked, the main grouch being that because the rate for the work was not good we were expected to overload by as much as four tons. Although at that time, there weren't the same Ministry checks a nowadays we did not agree, but it was best not to argue with Ken. One day Alan and I were on the rubber and drove to Liverpool docks together and started the usual hunt for the elusive checker to get a set under the correct hoist. If you were lucky, one could be found in 15 minutes but usually it took a tour of the whole quay to find the right one. This hurdle over and a checker secured it was usually time for the dockers first break. After the break the checker sometimes had to be found again before he would finally put you under a hoist. This particular day the dock was very busy and it was well into the afternoon before I got a set, Alan was put under the hoist behind me. The bales would come down at break neck speed from twenty odd feet above you and stop just short of the flat. As the bales had come thousands of miles in the hold of a ship, they were every conceivable shape and size, wedge shaped, rounded, fat and thin, a nightmare to load. You could land one that looked as though it had a good flat bottom only to find it rolled over too far out onto the chock rail. While struggling to sort that one out another bale would be hovering six inches above your head. The dockers would sometimes get a bit ratty with you but it was best to ignore them. Anyway, on this day it was after four in the afternoon before we were both loaded, I had about fourteen tons on and Alan eighteen, both well overloaded. As it was late afternoon, we arrived at the Leyland factory too late for unloading and rang Ken who exploded and said he needed us empty tonight. His next rave told us to roll them off outside the gates but when Alan told him we couldn't really do that he shouted "Get back here" and slammed the phone down. Back at the yard, he had another rant, which we both ignored and left for home. The next day we went the short distance to Leyland to unload which meant rolling the bales over the side where they bounced all over the place, one even smashed the rear light on Alan's lorry, it was a crazy way to unload but that was the norm so you just had to get on with it. Alan and I were getting a bit fed up of some of the things we had to do, indeed we both had said we would like to work for Ulster Ferry. Therefore, one day Alan and I took the plunge and asked the manager at U.F.T. if he had any vacancies for drivers. He sounded optimistic but didn't offer us anything, "Wait and see" were his words. We left the office a bit fed up and resolved to keep trying, we both felt that on the whole of the dock estate there must be something for us. Neither of us had been at Ditchfields very long, but my move from Bambers was purely financial and I never intended the job to be long term.

About a week later whilst loading at U.F.T. the foreman told me to go to the office as the manager wanted to speak to me. At the office, the manager said he was prepared to offer us both a job with the company, we could start in two weeks and I was to tell Alan to come and see him. I left the office in a dream, at last, I was to work for a bigger, better company. I hung around for Alan that night to tell him the news and he was in the same excited mood as I was. At home, Margaret was also very pleased, especially when I told her about the wage increase.

Alan and I both felt it best to give our notice in to Ken the next day, news that went down very, very badly especially as we would not say where we were going. Ken was to find out sooner than we thought, Ken was a good bloke, but I was just doing what I had to do.

CHAPTER TWO
THE IRISH CONNECTION

Alan and I arrived at the Ulster Ferry Transport compound just before 7am on a wet and windy Monday and were met by Jack Nightingale the foreman, he told us that for the time being we were to become dock shunters and help out under the crane until we went on the road. I was to drive an old bull-nosed Leyland Comet with a Scammell coupling. The majority of the dock trailers and a good proportion of the road trailers used this coupling method and there were not too many fifth wheel trailers around at U.F.T. As I had shunted the Austin artic around the yard at Parks and had also done the same at many farmyards I was in a better position than Alan as far as any experience of an artic went. Jack the foreman got me moving trailers in the shed right away, he even said that I was not bad, the lads in the shed also said I was better than the last shunter. At around 9.30, it was brew time and we all gathered in the small cabin near the crane. Jack introduced Alan and myself to the others and it felt good as we both knew most of them. Harry, a Dutchman, was the crane driver with Mick as his slinger. Hughie, a man in his 50s worked in the customs shed. In the warehouse was Jackie, a very small man also in his 50s who had two lads called Peter and Richard working under him.

After the break, Jack took Alan and I to one side to explain in more detail what was expected from us, beginning with the work we would be doing when the boats came in the dock. The boats that U.F.T. would have cargo on were operated by a company called Transport Ferry Services who had a large office building near the dock entrance. We would be expected to be at these ships with empty trailers and load any U.F.T. flats or containers. We could get a list from the office of what was arriving on that days tide, and on what ships the cargo was on. If there were enough empty trailers all these loads could be left on the trailers and parked in the shipping lanes as near as possible to the compound. If there was an empty trailer shortage, the loads had to be brought to the compound and the crane would take them off. Jack said it was a bit of a juggling act and we would have to be on our toes. As far as loads being shipped out we would again get a list, and that we should see the cargo inspectors at each berth to ascertain when he would need the loads. Most of the loads would be on trailers but some were likely to be under the crane and we would have to get them lifted. Finishing off Jack also explained we would have to move trailers in the transhipping shed as well as the customs shed and bring loaded trailers under the crane for transfer to U.F.T. vehicles as well as sub-contractors. Jack seemed a good foreman and a man you could work for and I did not foresee any problems.

The tide was late that day and we spent the morning moving trailers and assisting in the sheds, gradually getting better at reversing as the morning passed by. At dinner, we were inducted into the card school that needed Alan and I to make up the numbers. It was only seven card brag for pennies but as we saw, it soon built up into a fair pile. After dinner, I walked out of the cabin and nearly bumped into Ken, my old boss. Ken looked very mad, and when Alan walked out of the cabin, he was getting very angry and shouted to Jack that they could not take his drivers. Jack told him to go and see the manager and we heard later that Ken had lost the argument and our new manager had stood his ground. Ken got his load on and departed saying nothing to either of us.

The boats started arriving in the dock soon after dinner and Jack told me to be ready at the basin berth where the first boat usually docked. I watched it come through the outer lock gates and tie up alongside the crane. The boat was the M.V. LINDA a Dutch boat on charter to T.F.S. She was a very clean looking vessel, black with white uppers and a white stripe on her hull. Immediately the dockers went aboard and began taking the cables and shackles off the loads and within minutes, the crane had plucked a U.F.T. container off the deck. I could see other cargo that I would have to get back for, so once the container was landed; I was away to the lanes for a quick swap with an empty trailer. I got three containers and a flat off the top deck, luckily there were no more until the tween deck was opened. Jack stopped me and said there was a U.F.T. container hanging in the air at another berth, he told me quite calmly that I would have to be aware and that it would all come to me in time. His easy manner really meant something to me, and I was glad that he was the foreman. Alan was as busy as I was and saw him a few times but we couldn't stop to chat. The first boat to be empty was the basin boat, which was usually the case as I found out later, and by late afternoon, the boat was ready to re-load. As we had only a couple of heavy loads to go on the bottom deck, it was straightforward. As well as the basin boat, I had taken loads off two other boats including the BARDIC FERRY that was unloading up the ramp from her hold. The ferry carried cargo on her top deck and it was up to us to be there for these loads. Alan and I had a very busy day shunting the boats, bringing loads under the crane for sub-contractors and moving trailers in both sheds but I was really enjoying everything about the job.

As it was a late tide and U.F.T. had some light loads for top deck cargo, it was after eight pm when we clocked off and I arrived home tired but pleased. Margaret made my dinner and I told her about the day, she accepted that I was going to be late many nights and would be working seven days a week but liked the thought of no more money worries. Things at home were going alright and we seemed to be happy. There were a few things I didn't like, one of which was the too often visits of my mother-in-law, she was either there when I got home or arrived soon after, Margaret said I was ignorant because I didn't speak.

As my first week continued, everything started to click into place as Jack the foreman had said it would. I got to know everyone better and found out about my new work mates lives. Hughie was really known as "Fingers" as he had lost his middle finger on one hand when he trapped it in a shed door. He was his own boss in the customs shed, he had to search in containers for items the customs wanted to inspect as they had come from Southern Ireland. Harry, the Dutch crane driver was a very private man and did not say much, but a likeable man all the same. Mick, the crane slinger was a big man in his mid-twenties, very loud and a bit short tempered but as the weeks went by were getting along just fine. Jackie, the foreman in the transhipping shed was a worrier and got in a panic over trivial things, we helped him out by moving trailers as soon as required, this calmed him down a lot. I think he got worried if things were getting behind so a quick response from the shunters pleased him greatly. The two lads Peter and Richard worked in the shed with Jackie and were good company at break times. I got to know some of the office staff as we were always in and out for lists and manifest's. The shipping manager was Billy, a big happy man in his late 50s; Billy handled anything to do with cargo lists and manifest's. The dinnertime card school was always enjoyable, mainly because this was my first job where I could relax at set times with mates around. Mick in particular was a bit of a card shark, but we could always tell when he had a good hand as he would lean back in his chair into the door way of the other room, Hughie would shout "Mick has gone in the back room" when this happened.

The weeks flew by and Alan went on the road with his Leyland Comet, I think he was glad as he didn't seem to be settling on the docks, where as I was very happy with it all. I had no other plans but to go back on the road, but it did not work out like that. I was asked to go to the office to see the manager and Jack the foreman, thinking I had done something wrong, I was a little apprehensive about the summons. On entering the office, Jack smiled at me and I knew I had no worries. Jack started by saying that I could go on the road if I wished but they both felt that as I was good at the work on the docks even after such a short time, they would like me to stay on the docks as a permanent shunter. This really threw me, I wanted to go back on the road, but was being offered a job that I already grown to like. I think they saw my problem but when the manager said they liked my work and that I would be an asset on the docks I made my mind up in an instant. Jack told me another shunter would be taken on as Alan was now driving , I left the office feeling chuffed that I was valued and that I would be the main man as far as shunting went.

In the mid to late sixties Preston Docks was in the middle of its most profitable time since its opening. On the south side the imports where very varied, large amounts of wood pulp, timber, bananas, china clay and general cargoes. The banana boats where really handsome vessels and watching them turning in the dock was a lovely sight. Russian ships bringing timber were some of the largest ships to visit Preston; a couple of inches either side coming through the lock gates was all they had. All this traffic was a boom time for the local haulage industry with Addisons, BRS, Turners from Chorley and a host of others all having a share. On the north side coal was still being loaded at the old coal hoist. On the north side of the basin dock tankers were a regular sight delivering their oil to the storage facilities. However, it was the Irish traffic that was really shooting ahead. Apart from U.F.T., there was Northern Ireland Trailers, Anglo Irish, Ferrymaster, Containerway, Roadferry, Greenore and Seawheel. On the north side when the boats had arrived it was total chaos, sometimes if both ferries were in dock and were discharging from below, all the lanes were full, shunters were up and down to the different berths and mixed in with all this were the haulage contractor's lorries as well the shipping companies own vehicles.

The dockers themselves where a great crowd of men and already my two favourites where the basin gang slingers, especially a chap called Dick Vickers who was self-appointed foreman and had an abounding enthusiasm for getting the job done, he could make the whole gang work harder than the foreman could. The story went that Dick had an agreement with the captains of the two basin boats to be first up the river. The docks had its own tugboats and a small fleet of dredgers to keep the channel clear of sand and silt. It was a never ending battle for the dredgers and they were constantly at work. Some smart-alecs used to say all the sand that had been dredged came back in on the next tide as they did not go out to sea far enough, but I never really believed that.

Practically all the trailers we had to use on the docks had the Scammell couplings, some were road trailers but many were very old and not in good condition. U.F.T. had fifth wheel trailers but they were all road trailers which we would use for heavy loads off the boats.

As we had no fifth wheel shunt units the same as other companies, it meant using a detachable fifth wheel. It was usually left on the last fifth wheel trailer to be used and by carefully guiding the Scammell ramps into the guides on the coupling, it locked as a normal Scammell trailer would. Then by uncoupling the fifth wheel from the trailer it was attached to, it was then in place to pick a fifth wheel trailer up. The fifth wheel was about two inches too low for a trailer dropped by a road unit so it meant winding the trailer legs up and also letting the air out of the tank. It worked fine but sometimes it was a bit of a search to find the trailer it had been left on. Sometimes a very heavy load came off the boat out of turn, if I was there with a Scammell trailer, I had to take it, but with care it was not a problem on the docks.

The new shunter started work with me not long after my decision to stay on the docks, his name was yet another Alan and he was an ex-corporation bus driver aged about forty. He was a good bloke but after a week or so, nothing was sinking in and he already had a habit of disappearing for twenty minutes or so. That was fair enough when it was quiet but at busy tide times it was already annoying. However, we got along and I gave him the benefit of the doubt.

U.F.T. had a small fleet of lorries, half of which were Leyland Comets with Scammell couplings, the rest being Atkinson and powered by the Gardner 150 engine. To have an Atkinson was considered by some drivers to be a cut above the Leyland Comet drivers. There were about ten drivers and we did not see too much of them, occasionally a couple would be in the cabin at dinner time and listening to the stories about their travels made me sometimes regret my decision to stay on the docks. One particular driver called Mick, a man of about twenty five was a particularly exuberant character, when he came into the cabin the whole place reverberated with his loud voice. He considered himself to be top driver and let everyone know it. If the shunters were working late, we would sometimes use a fifth wheel road unit instead of the detachable one on the Leyland. If we used Mick's Atkinson, which we usually chose as we could flick through his girlie mags, he knew if his beloved Atkinson had been moved. Mick was in the cabin one dinnertime when he should have been long gone, suddenly Jack came in and told him to be on his way. Words were exchanged and Mick stormed out, got in his cab and shot down the quayside at the top of the lanes. Unfortunately, and unseen by him, a car transporter was unloading cars at the top of a lane with the top deck protruding past the end of the lane. Mick's cab went under the deck but the container on his trailer hit the top deck of the transporter. He was very lucky the transporter driver had finished unloading. It made a mess of the container and it certainly silenced Mick for a while.

All was going well, but every so often more flats and containers than usual would be shipped from Ireland and that meant we had to get trailers unloaded under the crane. We did not want to put the loads that were for shipping on the ground, as they needed to stay on the trailers. We did what we could, but as the boats started to unload, we had to get loads off under the crane, which took time especially if the crane was loading a sub-contractor. Inevitably, one or two berths were waiting for us with a load hanging on the crane. Occasionally the quayside foreman would land the flat or container on the quayside and carry on unloading. Usually get a re-lift incurred a fixed fee, but most foremen would lift the load for us once the boat was empty, and say nothing. The Scammell coupling on the shunt units took a lot of hammer and the S bar that activated the trailer dolly wheels got bent sometimes. When this happened, the trailer fell on its knees and had to be lifted back onto its landing wheels. The hand brake on the Scammell trailers was a simple ratchet affair that could be tightened with your foot, but even then the brake would not hold. If a trailer had been dropped in the middle of a lane instead of up to kerbs either side of the lanes it was possible to run at it with a bit of speed and hope it ran up the ramps and connected. Sometimes I had to chase it a bit, it was a bit dodgy and some shunters had chased trailers into the dock. The diver had to go down to put slings round the trailer; a quayside crane then lifted it out.

Towards the end of the year a very sad time in my life occurred. Margaret and I had gone to bed, it was around mid-night when we were woken up by heavy knocks on the front door. On going down and opening the door I was confronted by two police officers who asked could they come in. I showed them inside and by now, Margaret had come downstairs. One of the police officers began by saying they had brought bad news and there was no easy way to tell us. After a pause he told us that my father had died earlier in the evening. The news totally knocked me down and I did not know what to do or say. They said they had just come from mum's house and that my sisters were there and it would be easier if I went home the next day as mum had been sedated. After they had gone, it really sunk in and I didn't go to bed that night. After ringing work early the next morning, I set off to see mum. My sisters were with mum but as she was totally grief- stricken there was little I could do. The next few days were awful for everyone, one of the worst times of my life. Dad was a policeman in Preston, over six feet tall, fifteen stones, a red face and fifteen years a constable, an old-fashioned bobby. He had been a very young Merchant Navy officer on the convoys during the war and had survived all that to die at the age of forty-five. On the night of his death mum and dad had gone to the pictures to see 'The Dirty Dozen' and half way through dad told mum he felt ill, mum tried to help but dad had collapsed in his seat, mum told me later she knew he was already dead. That was dad's third heart attack and this one had proved to be fatal. The funeral was a solemn sort of majestic day with a policeman at every road junction and policemen in lines at some places, all saluting as dad's coffin passed by.

Of all the people I have known dad is the one I miss the most, I still do today over forty six years later, if there is an afterlife I hope to see him again. R.I.P. DAD (William Whitfield)

As they say "Life goes on" but for a long time after I thought of dad every day, still think of him a lot even now. However, mum was left alone with my two brothers, Chris the youngest was only five years old at the time.

Once back at work, and even though I was with my mates it was hard getting back into the swing of things. U.F.T. had purchased some new forty-foot trailers along with some twenty-foot tandems to take the new I.S.O. containers, they all had twist-locks and the forty foot ones had eight in total. The trouble was that the shipping lanes were not very wide and it was a struggle getting them parked in some places, but they certainly helped the shunters as we could now get two loads at a time from the boats. A forty-foot trailer with two containers on looked a bit odd behind a Leyland Comet, but as we were not blessed with tug-masters and hydraulic fifth wheels like other companies we used what we had. Back in the late 1960s, the I.S.O. containers were being carried on lorries that were totally unsuitable and very dangerous. We loaded these containers onto the lorries and trailers, but the problem was that the containers where too wide to fit inside the chock rail, they had to be raised on timber or any bits of wood the drivers could find. Watching the crane lowering a heavy container onto a lorry and seeing the flat bend and give, scared me even then. At the time, there was no legislation to stop this practice and practically all the sub- contractors had no twist locks fitted. The bad practice was compounded by the containers being fastened to the lorry flat or trailer by nothing more than rope through each corner of the container.

As well as the new trailers, a new shunt unit came for me from Liverpool. It was a newer model Leyland Comet that as well as having the normal Scammell coupling,was fitted with a movable fifth wheel. With the fifth wheel raised up and flat to the back of the cab it was used for Scammell coupling trailers. By using a switch in the cab, the fifth wheel lowered to rest on top of the Scammell coupling, after use it was raised to the back of the cab again. It would not lift trailers but made the messing around with the detachable fifth wheel a thing of the past. The fifth wheel was still a bit low and no amount of asking the drivers to drop their trailers a couple of inches lower altered the fact that I had to wind the trailer legs up a bit.

At the weekends, work really increased with meat containers and trailers of eggs coming off the boats on both days. The trailers with the eggs on went to Jackie in the shed as he had some complex transhipping to do on the loads. Sometimes it meant moving three or four trailers around to make it as easy as possible for Jackie and the lads; we had to find the time somehow, as well as seeing to the boats and the many sub- contractors that arrived at weekends. Many small, long gone haulage contractors and owner-drivers came at weekends for the meat containers and flats of eggs, one such contractor was Bradleys of Accrington with their unusual International units. Their drivers would leave empty trailers on the docks and I would catch the correct containers off the boats for them. It saved us all time and when their shunter arrived on Sundays, some of his job was done. At least Bradley's trailers were wide enough to take an I.S.O. container, but no twist locks were fitted.

One U.F.T. driver who was supposed to travel on Sunday went home instead, and all would have been well but at 2am on Monday morning, he came down Tulketh road in Preston and hit the low bridge severely damaging the container, predictably, he lost his job. Another driver went home and parked out-side a factory entrance thinking he would be long gone by the time the factory opened the next day. He overslept by a massive margin and at 7am the next day the lorry was still there causing the factory manager to ring our office, Jack had to go out with spare keys to move it, and then went round to the drivers house to sack him as well.

Alan, the new shunter and I were getting along fine, he was a bit slow and was still going missing every so often but as long as we got through I didn't mind doing a bit more than him. I was getting friendly with the dockers and liked working with them especially Dick of the basin gang. One docker, who I only ever knew as Sooty, drove a tug-master shunt unit and drove vehicles on and off the ferries. He was not a tall man but very broad and always had a smile for everyone. If any large or heavy loads were going on the ferries it was Sooty they sent for, he could drive anything and put trailers in some very difficult places inside the ferries. It was not the done thing for dockers to enter the compounds but Sooty was always willing to help, a few times he brought a load to the compound and got it lifted off to keep things moving, a great bloke who was a pleasure to know. There were one or two to be wary of and a particular one upset me as the ferry was unloading. I had shouted to him as he was dumping trailers in the middle of our unofficial trailer lane. He dived out of his cab and flew at me looking very menacing. He was a huge man and I thought my end was coming, but luckily, he thought better about flooring me and just told me to watch it. In time we became very good friends and on first name terms.

We were having good times on the Irish traffic in the late sixties, all the shipping companies were extremely busy and making money. At U.F.T. every one of the depot staff was making big wages with the shunters at the top of the money list. I was now used to working seven days a week with the odd day off and days of twelve to fourteen hours were the norm, indeed on some days especially on late tides it got longer than this. We still had the same problems but by now, Alan and I could work our way out of any difficult situations. When there was not an empty trailer to be found anywhere and we were really pushed, I would borrow (without asking) another companies trailer, we were always short of trailers and it was a real problem if the crane was busy. Sometimes I would sneak around the back of the NIT compound past Greenore Ferry to avoid being seen, it was best not to do it too often though. The sub- contractors that U.F.T. used were mostly local companies including Ditchfields, Bradleys, Rawcliffes, Sutcliffes, Mertrons and many other small and one-man haulage firms. When unloading the sub- contractors it was best to put the flat or container onto a trailer as it was easier when it came time for it to be shipped. If empty trailers were scarce, Harry the crane driver would surround the crane with empty and loaded flats and containers, sometimes stacking the containers two high. The very heavy loads had to be lifted on a straight up and down basis; these heavy loads nearly always went on a trailer. The crane was a very old Scotch derrick crane that Harry said was once powered by steam. It had about a seventy odd foot jib and could lift over twenty tons. When jibbed out Harry had to be careful not to over-extend the crane, the old girl soon let him know when he was asking too much of her. The shunters helped Mick under the crane with the shackling and manoeuvering loads especially when it was windy. The dinner time card school was a good break and Hughie covered a board with green felt and bought us a new pack of cards, the old ones were like blankets.

A couple of new ERF with 180 Gardner engines arrived and one was to go on a new trunk service to Watford Gap were the driver was to change over with a London Tooley St. driver. The trunk would also be using the forty-foot trailers that had arrived recently. We had to get this trailer ready for him by six thirty or so and the chosen driver didn't like waiting around. In addition, also to arrive with the new ERFs were a couple of Ford D series Custom Cab units with fifth wheel couplings, Alan my mate from Ditchfields was to get one of these units.

It was on a Sunday morning that a big disaster occurred at U.F.T. and it involved my old Ditchfield Dodge. The Dodge had come under the crane to collect a meat container and Harry was lowering it onto the lorry, but as the doors were the wrong way round I jumped onto the lorry flat to turn the container which was a few feet above my head. Suddenly there was a tremendous sound of tortured steel and breaking metal. Mick screamed at me to get off and I was a few yards away when the meat container smashed down onto Ditchfield's lorry, this was followed by a roaring sound and the crane jib, all seventy odd foot of it came crashing down. The end of the jib landed right on the cab roof of a Northern Ireland Trailers Leyland Comet that was waiting to have its trailer checked at the N.I.T. shed next to us. Practically the whole dock stopped and people came running from all over. It could have been the end of me, Mick, Harry and Freddie the N.I.T. driver but we all escaped. Harry the crane driver was very shocked and did not leave the crane cabin for a good five minutes. He said later pieces of cogs flew past his head and smashed the back of the crane cabin. It was unknown to me at the time but Freddie the N.I.T. driver was to become a good mate later in my next job.

For the rest of the day the lifting of flats and containers from trailers to contractors was done in other compounds, which took forever as it was Sunday, the busiest day of the week. A Chris Miller mobile crane arrived after dinner to move the crane parts out of the way and to stay with us to lift loads off the floor and load transfers. The Chris Miller crane stayed with us for a few days and we had heard a rumour that we were getting a mobile crane of our own. The crane arrived later in the week and we were all a bit shocked by the age of it. The mobile crane had four axles and the usual half cab for the driver, the crane driver's cab being set alongside the base of the jib. We set to with Harry and Mick constructing the jib and Harry elected to have as long a jib as possible so that empties and light loads could be jibbed further out of the way. Because of the crane out-riggers, a lot of room was needed to work in and to allow the crane to be moved up and down the compound. Once set up Harry did some test lifts to get the hang of operating the crane and admitted that despite its age the crane was very good.

From then on, we felt obliged to assist Mick with the crane especially as every time a move was made the crane had to be blocked under the out-riggers and then the screw jacks tightened up. It all took time and was very heavy work but as we all worked well together it somehow made it feel easier. The crane could lift heavy loads with ease, but only as straight up and down lift. As far as jibbing out was concerned, it was surprising how far Harry dared to go. It was essential though, that the crane was blocked up correctly to avoid any mishaps. A couple of weeks later a two axle Seddon rigid belonging to Jack Keany with a Lancashire flat on came in to be unloaded, the driver told Mick it was about ten tons. Trying to do the lift in one slewing movement Harry jibbed out to be able to place the flat on the ground a little way off and save unblocking the crane, as he started to lift, the front of the crane rose and the two front axles were almost off the ground when Harry lowered the load back onto the lorry. When we checked the notes, it was found the flat had sixteen tons of boxed nails on it. The driver said it had been a struggle up all the hills and made funny noises on corners, "nailed to the road" so to speak. Many of the sub-contractors sometimes hadn't a clue what weight they had on their lorries, so Harry said from now on he would treat most loads as heavy and set up accordingly. We thought Harry was still getting over the trauma of the big crane's collapse and did not want any more accidents. He had told us that he had seen mobile crane accidents and quite rightly took his and our safety seriously. Considering the age of our crane it performed remarkably well, over twenty ton loads were lifted with ease. Harry was able to sit down to operate this crane, he was standing all day with the old Scotch derrick crane, plus the controls were a lot easier to operate. The old crane had massive levers that had to be moved many times when performing all its different manoeuvres. The old crane was over ninety years old when it met its end, it must have done a lot of work in its long life.

Our work at U.F.T. was increasing all the time and new equipment was arriving regularly, especially new trailers and containers. The weekend meat and egg traffic from Ireland had increased a great deal and all this was welcome, as everyone deep down prefers working with a successful company. Jack Nightingale, our foreman was the best bloke I had ever worked for; he made the work run smoothly, trusted people, he was always ready to help us with advice and worked hard himself. He would let us go to Bills café for the morning break bacon sandwiches and sometimes we would have our dinner at the cafe or maybe visit the seaman's mission on the docks for a sandwich, in those days there were no mobile snack bars and cafes flourished.

In September of 1968, Margaret gave birth to baby boy in Sharoe Green hospital and both were well. I had a week off work in time for their arrival home; the first days off I had taken in nine months. I knew Margaret wanted her mum there and it didn't bother me, as I was not at work and therefore a bit more tolerant. We decided to christen him David and we all had a good week.

I was soon back into the work and was glad to see everyone again even though I was secretly missing home. In October of that year the Acrilan warehouse at Northern Ireland Trailers on the edge of the dock was destroyed by a massive fire, one of the biggest in Preston for many years, it must have caused tremendous problems for N.I.T. but as they were such a big company, they recovered quickly.

Christmas was approaching and a mate at Anglo Irish called Norman put forward the idea of a night out for some of the depot staff from different companies on the docks, and such was the response we had soon enough names to fill a coach. We decided to have our boy's night out at the Miami Bowl, a large nightspot in Morecambe. We all paid Norman a bit of money for a few weeks to cover the cost of the coach hire. We had all forewarned our bosses of the date of the trip and when the day came, everyone made the coach, which was a remarkable achievement. On arrival at the Miami Bowl and after a drink or two, we were all in party mood. I do not think I have ever laughed as much in my life as I did that night, as mates and people I knew just to nod at turned out to be great company. The compere knew who we were and announced over the microphone "When are the lads from Preston docks going to get with the girls from K Shoes from Kendal". That was the signal for many of us to start having an even better time and the evening flew by until it was time to go home. Most of us on the trip had to be back at work the next morning in time for the usual weekend rush.

I was at work on time on the Saturday morning and as far as I knew, no one missed turning up even though many of us were feeling pretty awful, but as the day went on, I was feeling a lot better than I did at 6am.

During the winter months, the Irish Sea was a very stormy sea and the smaller boats suffered badly. Most would shelter in Douglas Bay until the worst was over, but flats and containers were lost overboard on quite a few occasions. We used to go to the bull-nose at the basin dock and watch the smaller boats coming up the river listing badly, once docked and the tween deck hatches opened, it could be seen that the loads on the flats had shifted and were hanging in the sheets. This made a lot of work for the dockers, as they had to re-load the flats prior to lifting. Some of the U.F.T. flats had very wide shackling lugs which the dock shackles were too narrow to fit, we had one set of wide shackles for use by the dockers and this caused problems. It was usually the case that more than one berth rang us via Transport Ferry Services to inform us they required the shackles. Usually it meant searching the other berths to find them thrown on the quayside and then making a quick dash to deliver them, hoping it was not the basin gang we were holding up. The management refused to buy another set saying that they would get lost so we had to manage with the one set.

That year the Hong Kong Flu virus that had started in the Far East the previous year swept the U.K. The flu decimated the depot staff and at one time, for a few days, there was only Jack and I to run everything. The manager told us to do what we could and for a few nights, empty trailers were arriving from Liverpool to make it a bit easier for us. The virus affected many companies on the dock, but Jack and I escaped the infection much to the manager's relief. It took a few weeks to clear up but was very serious for many people in Great Britain.

Around this time there was a strike in Ireland and no cement was being produced anywhere. We were shipping some cement from Ribble Cement at Clitheroe and we had quite a few loads awaiting shipment. Then someone in Ireland came up with a plan to make money out of the shortage, a good plan if no one found out.

Old artics were being bought in England and the drivers brought them to Ulster Ferry were they began to unload the cement off the flats awaiting shipment onto the old lorries, which was fair enough, but incredibly they were loading two twenty ton loads onto the old artics. Sooty was putting one of the loads on the ferry and it nearly ran away with him. I don't think the ferry company condoned the practice and a few loads had been shipped like this before Transport Ferry Services put a stop to the dangerous practice.

In the late sixties the dockers at Preston went on strike, a strike that was to last a long time. At first U.F.T. in Liverpool handled the extra work, but at Preston things were very quiet and coupled with the loss of overtime we were getting a bit bored. At eight hours a day and no overtime, it cost most of us half our wages. Then in the third week, we heard that U.F.T. along with some of the other companies were to start shipping out of Heysham. The plan was for the drivers and shunters, including myself, to ferry loads to Heysham and a shunter was to stay at Heysham to unload and reload our cargo. My role was to stay at Heysham and every afternoon I took a unit usually with a forty-foot trailer loaded with two containers or flats to the Port. The work at Heysham was very slow and it took twice as long for the dockers to do a lift on or off the boat and the job was forever stopping and starting, it didn't flow smoothly as it did at Preston. When departing from Preston dock there was a certain amount of agro at the dock gates from groups of dockers and I seem to remember the police stopping the traffic to allow everyone to stream out without stopping. My overtime shot back up as it was in the early hours of the morning by the time I arrived back at Preston with two loads on the trailer. The trips to Heysham were making me a bit restless and it crossed my mind to go back on the road but I suppressed it for the time being. After ten weeks, the strike was over and whilst I had been earning good money, it was not doing my marriage any good and I hardly saw the children, Margaret got most things she wanted for the house but we seemed to be drifting a bit. I used to say that I was first out of Bamber Bridge in a morning and last back in at night. My neighbour, when I saw him, would comment on how much money I must be earning , I usually replied that I was working more than double his hours every week and I would get him a job with us, needless to say he declined my offer.

Normality returned to the dock and there was no animosity shown to us by the dockers, I thought they were glad to be back at work after the long strike. Mick also was glad to be back to normal and could start being on time for work as during the strike I could not pick him up on my way to the docks. He was a bit of a pain sometimes especially when on arriving at his house he would still be in bed. I had to leave home earlier to allow for this, he insisted I had a cup of tea while he made himself a bacon sandwich. Mick was the opposite of me as I have always been too early for everything and hated being late, but what can you do when it is a workmate. Ulster Ferry had joined with Link Line from Liverpool and we were getting quite a lot of their flats and containers arriving at Preston, we also gained a decent amount of Link Line trailers that helped us greatly. A couple of AEC Mercury road units arrived for the drivers at Preston, they were not new but were in excellent condition, the drivers who got them thought them to be very good, certainly better than the Fords they had been driving. Link Line drivers came to Preston, most of them still driving TK Bedford's with Scammell couplings. I think they only used the Bedfords for local work and we never saw any of their better lorries at Preston. The Mercurys that came to Preston had the "Ergomatic" cabs, the Mercurys used in Liverpool were the earlier version with the Park Royal cab, and we got one of these for dock use at Preston. Alan my co-shunter elected to drive the Mercury, and I carried on with dual coupling Comet.

When we had a quiet time we spent it gathering empty trailers together, sorting loads out under the crane and generally getting ready for the rush as the boats came in. We did get some time to drive around the docks chatting to other shunters and dockers, sometimes even sneaking off to the seamans mission for a cup of tea, Jack, our foreman never asked where we had been, I think he accepted that our work rate at busy times entitled us to a bit of easy time now and again. Our depot manager was a different kettle of fish though, he tended to be very aloof and we got the impression that he was always watching us and did not really trust us. The work everyone on the docks got through was incredible, the hours worked sometimes amounted to double that of a factory or office worker but everyone was always cheerful, it could get a bit stressful and sometimes it was best to keep out of the way of one or two certain shunters or dockers, but on the whole it was a good working environment and it was certainly an interesting place to be. For myself the best time was watching the bigger ships entering the docks especially if they had the tug boats with them.

1954 LEYLAND COMET
PHOTO BY GRAHAM ROBERTSON

ULSTER FERRY LEYLAND COMET
PHOTO COURTESY OF NA3T ARCHIVE OF TRANSPORT
TRAVEL AND TRADE

Things were changing at Ulster Ferry, Jack gained promotion to equipment supervisor, a move that was not going benefit us. The first to step up and try the foreman's job was Hughie, he was a cracking bloke but totally unsuited to the job. Hughie liked a drink and never wanted to do much overtime, especially when his favourite club on the Larches estate was open, consequently he was missing when Jack would have been there. He was not a young man, his hideout in the customs was his private world, and I think he missed the peace. However, Alan and I virtually ran our side of the job, and shunting to and from the boats was by now never a real problem.

Other companies on the docks seemed to be just as busy, but Northern Ireland Trailers, in the same business as U.F.T, had by far the most work and the best equipment. The amount of new vehicles, equipment and buildings was staggering especially compared to Ulster Ferry; we appeared to be the poor relations of the dock. The one thing we were getting was a new compound, it was on Chaincaul Road alongside the N.I.T. maintenance bays and compound. It was a long way from the quayside and the basin dock and we could foresee difficulties in the move.

We eventually moved in to our new compound, it was a huge area compared to our cramped spot near the top end of the dock. On the right of the gate was the depot staff building and on the left was a good-sized block of single storey offices. Half the compound was tarmaced and the rest covered with large chippings on a hard base. Harry tested this area and deemed it fit for the crane, the large area meant that we could put containers and flats on the ground in orderly lines.

THE GOODWILL TRAVELLER LOADING AT PRESTON
PHOTO COURTESY OF WILLIAM WRIGHT

OTHER BOATS THAT VISITED PRESTON
DORIC FERRY
IONIC FERRY
BARBEL BOLTEN
WIRRAL COAST
MARIETTA BOLTEN
DORSET COAST
MOYLE
ELISA
LINDA
SOLWAY FISHER

THE GOODWILL TRAVELLER AND THE BARDIC FERRY
PHOTO COURTESY OF WILLIAM WRIGHT

DORIC FERRY
PHOTO BY CLYDEBUILT DATABASE

ORWELL FISHER

The misgivings we had about the distance to the quayside soon became a reality, as when the boats were in dock and discharging their cargo the dock suffered from a lot of congestion, to travel from the new depot through this traffic , being slowed by drivers reversing their trailers into gaps made it even worse. Taking loads to and from the boats on dock use only trailers was a bit hazardous to say the least. We had to very careful when turning, as the flats and containers were never secured to the trailers; many were the twenty-foot Scammell type and grossly over-loaded. There had been mishaps in the past and so we drove with a bit of intrepidation some of the time.

The offices at the compound were inline with our rest rooms and it felt that we were being watched all the time, even working in the compound helping with the crane we felt the same, faces at windows, watching us do all the graft. One day Harry had an idea to stack the empty containers in a line to block us off from the office. Within a week, we had enough empties to complete our wall and even though the manager did sneak up on us sometimes, it was a lot better. When it was raining, it was completely safe because office staff do not like getting wet or cold. When the weather was really bad and in quiet periods we had an empty container placed with the doors open, near to our fire in an old oil drum. I think most of us would have preferred to stay at the old compound, it was a bit rough and ready but it's location at the centre of things was a lot easier all round. Our old cabin was not in view of the office, we hadn't got decent chairs, no table and our toilets were in the N.I.T. trailer bay next door but it was home all the same. There was a noticeable change of atmosphere and a certain change of familiarity between the office staff and the depot staff, it was not something I particularly liked and a few others held the same view.

The move increased the shunters workload tremendously but we were never asked about how things were going, Jack our old foreman still came for a chat sometimes but as he was now usually the manager's shadow even he had changed. About this time I was given a week's suspension for bringing a wrong flat under the crane for transfer to a sub-contractor. I was under pressure on that day and the driver never checked the flat number either, I thought it very unfair and even Jack was sympathetic. Luckily I got a week's work driving a Keanys eight legger Foden.

THE BARDIC FERRY AT PRESTON
PHOTO COURTESY OF WILLIAM WRIGHT

DORSET COAST

The Dorset Coast was one of the small boats that Anglo Irish Transport used to ship containers and flats to Ireland. The Anglo Irish compound was next to the N.I.T. offices and although the compound was very small they handled a tremendous amount of work. They had a gantry crane which was a lot easier to use than our Scotch derrick and mobile crane. Eddie Black the main man at Anglo caught me pinching his trailers a few times and waved his fist at me as I flew past their compound. He never got to upset about it and was always ready to help us with lifts under their crane, especially when our crane collapsed. A great bloke called Norman worked at Anglo and I became very good friends with him during my time on the docks, it was Norman who organized our night out at Morecambe.

BARBERS TRANSPORT AT THE BARDIC FERRY
PHOTO COURTESY OF WILLIAM WRIGHT

Barbers Transport were regular visitors to Ulster Ferry delivering egg trays from Great Yarmouth. This particular driver must have collected an empty flat on his last visit as usually we had to unload them onto our flats on the docks. When we were busy, they had to wait hours especially when three or four loads arrived at the same time, but they were a good bunch and were very patient with us

Margaret finally got her bigger new house in 1970, a newly built semi in Farrington Leyland that had three bedrooms, central heating and a brick garage, all for £3950. I had recently bought a Ford Capri, Margaret had a Singer Chamois, and all achieved with only my wage. It was definitely the best of times for everyone on the docks in the late sixties and early seventies.

Hughie lost his foreman's job, so it was back to the customs shed for him. Deep down he was relieved, he was not cut out to be a foreman and preferred the sanctuary of his shed. Little Jackie was next to take up the challenge and from day one he worried about everything and nothing, even though we gave him our full support. Over the next few months, for me at least, things were changing too much, and again I was getting restless. Driving past the Northern Ireland Trailers compounds all day long did not help, and in the end I was determined to go back on the road. I knew a foreman at N.I.T. called Jimmy Fowler and spoke to him about my chances of getting a start. Jimmy told me to go to the office and fill out an application form, which I did later that day. At the office, they told me that they would let me know and was rather disappointed not to get a better response. I saw Jimmy later in the day and he told me to come back to the office with him, and after he had spoken to the manager, I had a job, I was to start in two weeks. Thanking Jimmy for his help, I immediately gave my notice in at U.F.T. which was met with indifference by the manager but Jack Nightingale our ex foreman was quite shocked and said I would be greatly missed.

My next hurdle was to tell Margaret my news and she was not pleased at all, but in my mind, it was a good move for me and at the right time in my life. My defence was that I was the one going out to work and that it was what I really wanted. The next two weeks passed very slowly and I was glad when my last day came. My time at U.F.T. had been good and I had enjoyed working on the docks. U.F.T. had been good to me and I had repaid them with a lot of hard work, it was time to go.

CHAPTER THREE
BACK ON THE ROAD AGAIN

My first day at Northern Ireland Trailers was not a great strain as the first days in a new job usually are, I knew most of the depot staff and some of the drivers and so it was quite relaxed. It was a bit strange being next door to Ulster Ferry, I had been very happy with my job at that company but this was where I wanted to be. On the first day, two other drivers started and we were all told that as there were no units available we had to work in the depot for a while. We worked in the Acrilan warehouse and the bacon bay, in the second week I did some shunting to and from the boats, using one of the old Scammell units that had a lifting fifth wheel, it felt a bit weird, especially when I saw the U.F.T. shunters. After completing the week, Jimmy asked if I wanted to stay on the dock and be a N.I.T. shunter, but I was not falling for that again and politely refused. On Monday of the third week we were told that new drivers had to do a few days with the instructor on the training vehicle. We all had our H.G.V. licences but as N.I.T. was a modern company they were putting the training policy in place. As I had not been on the road very much in the last three and a half years, I was a bit nervous, but all went well and I got a good report at the end of the three days. I worked the rest of the week in the depot and on the Friday found out that units were available after the weekend, at last we were to start driving. I spent the weekend wondering what I would be driving, and where I would be going. The Monday came and at just before 7am I entered the traffic office and waited to get my notes amongst a crowd of other drivers. I saw a friendly face in the crowd, it was Freddie who's unit had been crushed in the U.F.T. crane accident and he came over to me and wished me luck. At the office window, I got my notes and keys and went into the compound to find my unit. I walked down the line of already hooked up units and trailers until I found my reg. number. It was an E.R.F. with a 150 Gardner engine, and looked very smart in the distinctive N.I.T. livery. The inside of the cab was very clean and tidy and I was very pleased my new lorry. N.I.T. looked after all their fleet not just with maintenance and tyres but the general appearance of every unit. All the trailers were checked before leaving the docks and loads changed over if there was any problem, all this gave everyone a degree of confidence about the company. I think N.I.T. was leading the way in many aspects of road transport and were probably one of the most go-ahead outfits in the country at the time. It was very pleasing to think that after a roundabout journey, I was at last back on the road with a large reputable company, it was made even better as I was no stranger to many of my new work mates.

My first job was only to Michelin at Burnley but it gave me a quiet day to become used to the ERF and my new job. It was going to take a few weeks to get used to the job and I was happy to take it slowly at first. The first week was spent on local work and I got through it reasonably well, but being on local work meant hardly any overtime and after my big wages at U.F.T. I had to try to get somewhere near to that amount. It was therefore pleasing, when on Friday night I found that I was going away on the

Sunday. All drivers at N.I.T. had to carry their overnight case with them at all times as there was no such thing as local drivers, you could be sent out again up to three or four o'clock in the afternoon. At home that weekend I gathered everything I would need and put them in a small suitcase in readiness for Sunday.

PHOTO COURTESY OF NA3T ARCHIVE OF TRANSPORT
TRAVEL AND TRADE

It was about 11am on the Sunday when I arrived at the docks and received my delivery notes. I was to deliver a load of baled bacon of which N.I.T. had a large contract to ship the bacon from Ireland. The bales where wrapped in hessian, held together with thin rope and weighed about one and a half hundredweight. My load was multi-drop and was to start at Witney and then onto Reading, Basingstoke, Southampton, Portsmouth finishing in Southsea. The load was on a newish thirty foot flat, mounted on a thirty foot skeletal trailer, and was sheeted and roped quite tidily. After checking everything, I set off for the motorway to head south. As the M5 was not all linked up at the time so by using a bit of the A46 and

A435 to Cheltenham I was able to join the A40 to Witney. After a couple of stops, I arrived in Witney around five o'clock and as I had bought the little red book that listed transport digs I stopped to sort this out. This was my first time away and was not sure when and where to ring for a bed but was happy to achieve my aim with my first call, and was told where to park up and given directions for the digs. As far as I can remember the chosen digs were satisfactory which as I was to find out later, was not always the case.

Most of the bacon drops where to Danish Bacon Company depots where the bales were usually rolled onto the shoulder of the staff at the depot. The bales were very heavy but they must have been used to it as it was no problem for them. At Sainsburys in Basingstoke I had to hang around for hours even though I was not in the general queue, eventually I was unloaded, the bales being stacked on pallets. All the bales were different grades and from different suppliers in Ireland so I had to be careful not to get my deliveries mixed up. By Wednesday dinnertime I was empty and rang Preston to find out what to do next. They told me to go to a place near Membury and pick up a load of empty stillages for Preston. After loading at Membury, I drove as far as Swindon where my time was almost up. Digs were easy to find, I found them quite reasonable, and after a good dinner, I just watched the television until bedtime. I not yet had into the habit of going out in an evening, a thing I would do more of later. The next day after stopping at Stoke depot for fuel, I arrived back at the docks where I was told to move a few trailers and generally make myself useful until home time. As I had started my week on Sunday, I knew that I would not be going far the next day, which was Friday.

On arriving home the in-laws car was in front of the house, so I decided to go straight in anyway. It didn't appear to me that I had been missed and especially with my in-laws there, I felt a bit deflated. They finally left after an hour or so, I told Margaret about my trip, and she generally seemed interested. The next day I took a load to Michelin at Stoke and returned with a loaded trailer from Stoke depot. My week was over, I had my overtime, and was looking forward to the weekend at home.

The weeks were going by and while I was a new starter, it felt better all the time. I knew a lot more drivers and got on well with most of them. One or two I was a bit wary of, Freddie said not to bother about them as there were a few old women working at N.I.T. and just to do my job and he would keep me right. Apart from Freddie Taylor, the many other drivers I became friendly with included, Bob Wright, Ray Skupski, Bert Wright, Bernard Cooper, George Tweedie, Gunnar Plits and many other great blokes who all made it a very friendly place to work.

One particular week I had returned to the docks at dinnertime and was told I was going away after dinner. Along with another driver, we were going to Birds Eye at Grimsby. We were each taking an insulted container mounted on short 4inline trailers. The plan was to get to Grimsby and load frozen food the next morning and be back that day so the loads could be in Ireland as soon as possible. At this time the M62 was not even open as far as Huddersfield, it was necessary to travel via Whalley and Todmorden so journey to Grimsby was a long tortuous route and seemed to take forever. The next day whilst being loaded I was amazed to see the other driver place a little pillow on his steering wheel, and after leaning forward he placed his head on the pillow. He was fast asleep in no time and I wished I could sleep that easily. On the return journey, I followed the other driver and was a bit shocked to see, on many occasions, especially on bad roads, the swaying of the container. The 4inline trailer lifted one of its narrow axles a tiny bit off the road, it always steadied itself but those particular trailers were not very stable and I was wary of them in the future.

The fleet at N.I.T. consisted of ERF units with 150 and 180 Gardner engines, others with Cummins and Rolls Royce engines and one with a Perkins engine. The Atkinson were mostly 6x2 rear steer's with one Chinese 6x2. They had one Foden two stroke, which sounded a real beast when it was running, lastly and I have saved the best until now, was the Atkinson Borderer with Cummins 205 engine. Apart from the four-inline trailers the rest were all-modern and innovative, including tri-axle rear steer skeletal trailers. Many new twenty and thirty foot I.S.O. flats had been recently purchased, so on the whole the fleet was one of the best in the country. The livery chosen for the fleet was very eye catching and unusual for the period.

Practically every driver had to take turns at starting the week on a Sunday, most wanted to do this and I was no different, it started the week with overtime for one thing. N.I.T. had a depot at Canning Town in London and a handful of Sunday drivers usually travelled to this depot. We all stayed at the Silvertown Motel that had bunk beds in the rooms, but as was a very popular place it was best to book a bed early. At the depot they could sometimes keep you there for a couple of days helping the cockneys, I never liked doing this as it cut the overtime down. Preston drivers always seemed to get more drops than the London drivers did, but we always got them done despite the London traffic.

Many of the loads we delivered into Yorkshire were bales of Acrilan that had come from Monsanto in Ireland. Before the M62 had reached Huddersfield a load of Acrilan with 2 or 3 drops and a backload was always a night out, but when the M62 opened to Huddersfield we were expected back. The return loads from Yorkshire varied, including many loads of clay pipes collected at Hepworth near Holmfirth on the A616 between Sheffield and Huddersfield. Another large job every so often was loading coils of steel wire at the Templeborough Rolling Mills in Rotherham. The wire was destined for Michelin in Ireland and up to twenty loads would be handled in a few days. Near the mills was one of the better digs, run by a couple who I think had been in the police. They would never turn a N.I.T. driver away and on some occasions took a driver or two home with them if the digs were full. As many as eight or nine N.I.T. drivers could be booked in, some of us even hung around at the mills just to be able to stay there. Dinner and breakfast served on a shift system in the kitchen and was worth the wait. As you can imagine, a crowd of drivers from the same company and all at the same digs meant a lot of laughs and larking about. Bert Wright who was quite a bit older than most of us, was the best company ever and it really was hilarious sometimes. After dinner and a wash, all of us would go to the local pub and take over the saloon bar. Bert was even better company with a drink inside him, we all had a great night every time in Rotherham. After the pub we went to the best fish and chip shop in Yorkshire and took the suppers back to the digs where the owners had left bread and brewing stuff out for us all. They really were great digs and great times, don't think it is like that nowadays. It was around this time street parking for lorries without lights had become law, it was to signal the end of some digs, especially the ones that were a good distance from a lorry park. We used to stay at some good digs off Leeds Road in Huddersfield, one morning we found large stickers on our windscreens saying "No street parking for lorries without lights". We did later, try taking a load of bulbs out of the trailer to avoid a flat battery, but it was too much messing around and that was the end of those digs for us. Doncaster was an excellent town for parking and the digs; it must be a Yorkshire thing. The lorry park was on the market after it closed in the late afternoon, the digs being mostly in one street very near the lorry park. One particular transport digs was on the right hand side of the street, cannot remember the name but it could have put some boarding houses to shame.

My ERF was plodding along at just over forty mph, but it was reliable and in good condition. When it was warm weather the cab would get hot from the heat of the engine and my back and legs were wet with perspiration, the small accelerator pedal felt like it was burning a hole in your boot as you tried to squeeze another one mph out of the engine.

It was after being at N.I.T. for a while that I had a fall at work, which at the time felt minor, but was to have serious consequences over the next few months and even up to the present time.

That particular day, after loading pallets of cans at Metal Box Westhoughton I was finishing off the roping at the back of the trailer, when a rope I was tightening suddenly snapped. I fell backwards and hit the back of my head on the concrete, I felt a bit shaken but otherwise none the worse, or so I thought. About two weeks later, I started to lose some movement in my left hand, my writing was very shaky, and I was losing some grip in the hand. Over the next couple of weeks, I had lost mobility in my left hand, arm and leg. By this time, I was off work and saw my doctor who sent me to hospital for tests.

It was serious now, I was dragging my left leg and could not walk properly, and I remember hurting my toes when going upstairs as my leg was just not lifting at all. At the time, scanners were in their infancy and at the hospital, they placed electrodes on my head to try to determine the cause of my paralysis. I saw a specialist through N.I.T. who along with the hospital doctors determined that I had damaged a blood vessel in my brain and there had been a small bleed. Margaret would drive me to the docks to take in my sick notes and I think everyone was genuinely concerned for me. After being on medication for a couple of months all my paralysis disappeared and I was ready to return to work after about three months off. Looking from then to present day, I have had other scans and one in 1985 showed another small bleed in my head and I now have a scan every two years. It led to my failing a medical in 1996 that put paid to being a H.G.V driver forever. I have also thought over the years my personality changed a bit since the accident.

On my return to work, I had been told to have light duties for a while but that is not possible when you are a lorry driver. I was asked if I wanted to work nights on the new trunk that was about to start from Preston to Frampton Cotterell the N.I.T. Bristol depot. The trunk was upsetting the shop stewards as they said the out and back journey was too far in one night. However the trunk started and instead of giving us both faster units I got a Borderer that did 50mph and my running mate was driving an ERF with a Rolls engine and did 60 mph. It was a bit of a slog at my 50mph and after two weeks the shop steward got the trunk stopped.

Therefore, I went back to my ERF and got back into the swing of the job quite easily. Not long after the shop steward and I went to a meeting in the office. It seemed that N.I.T had admitted that when the rope snapped and I had fallen, it was due to its use on bacon loads, which was rotting the rope. They offered me £500, which was a lot of money then, and the steward advised me to take it, which I did. N.I.T. employed a retired chap to look after and check the ropes in stock waiting to be used, a bit of an impossible job I thought.

One of the little perks that many drivers all over the country had, was to park up a reasonable distance from where they lived and get a lift home, thereby claiming the night out money. As I lived near to two motorway junctions, it was not really a problem for me, but for other N.I.T. drivers who lived in awkward places it could be difficult. Sometimes it took ages and a couple of lifts to get home, the next morning could be a challenge, especially in the dark. Many of us would park at Stoke depot and from the junction by the side of the depot we could make Preston in one lift. Odd times I had parked in the Stoke depot and after leaving my keys in the office and was just going out of the door a voice would shout "six in the morning." I think they did it for the fun of it, but it didn't bother me as the last N.I.T. trunks returning to Stoke the next morning crossed the motorway on a bridge near my house, and I was always back at Stoke on time.

Freddie, Bob and myself used to watch football at Preston North End and rarely missed a match, including some evening matches. Another good mate called Bernard Cooper and I were once staying in Darlington, from the bedroom window in the digs I spotted the flood lights on at Darlington's ground. I decided to go and see the match;

Bernard declined the pleasure saying I was a glutton for punishment.

Over the next few months, I had no problems at work but my home life felt a little strained. I was becoming increasingly restless and Margaret and I were not as close as we had been. I did feel more intolerant of things that in the past never bothered me, but all I could do was try to keep things together at home, maybe it was the accident or just me, I never found out really.

A Sunday arrived when it was my turn to work and I arrived at the compound around 10-30am or so. Looking down the row of units already hooked up to their loads, I could not see my ERF. On entering the traffic office, which was full of Sunday drivers I waited my turn to get to the window. Freddie was on the phone booking his bed at Silvertown and as I already knew that I was going to London asked him to book me in as well.

When I got to the office window, my notes and keys were handed to me, but they were not my ERF keys but the keys of a nearly new Atkinson Borderer that had the Cummins 205 engine. Some other drivers had spotted this and a cry of "Blue eyes" went up but I was not in the least bit bothered, I was to have a better unit at least for this trip. The Borderer, used by a driver who had just been sacked, was now a spare unit for the time being, his loss was my gain. I left the docks in high spirits and once Freddie and I were on the motorway I had the hang of the Fuller gearbox. We did have a brief training session on using the gearbox in the past and it had all come back to me.

Arriving at the London depot Freddie dropped his trailer and along with two other drivers, we went to the motel in his unit. After dinner and a wash and change, we all went to the local pub, which I think was the "Rose of

Denmark" where we spent a couple of hours. I have never been a big drinker and have always had to pace myself, drinking one pint to other peoples two or even three, in a way I took after my late father who did not drink at all.

The next two days I spent at Canning Town depot doing bacon drops around London, which by this time I was getting used to. Returning to Preston on the Wednesday of that week, I had one more night out in Yorkshire and finished the week with a local job. The Borderer was so much better than my old ERF, more power, better gearbox and looked a more attractive vehicle all round. This in mind, I plucked up the courage to ask in the office if I could keep the Borderer, I went straight to the top by asking Mr. Flett the manager and to my surprise and delight, he said "Yes". From then on, I had a love of the Atkinson Borderer especially when powered by the Cummins engine, I was to drive another in the future.

The offices at N.I.T were alongside the yard drivers used when booking in, most of the girls in the office were chatty, but some were a bit snooty. During hot weather, drivers had to enter the office suitably clothed, drivers had to put their shirts back on and generally anything that the management considered offensive to the women was frowned on. I think it was only the high and mighty that objected. The regime was a bit rigid but I suppose it was a sign of the times and larger companies had an image to project.

That summer wage negotiations had been taking place and were getting nowhere, so the shop stewards called for a union meeting. This took place on a Saturday evening in the union office on Strand Rd. near to the docks. The stewards and one or two drivers made speeches but the outcome was very uncertain, until one particular driver took centre stage, he was cockney and had the gift of public speaking. He gave us all such a blood and thunder speech that outcome of the meeting was never in doubt, there was to be a strike of all the drivers and depot staff.

The strike started very gently, but as the days past things got a bit out of hand. The flash point was the few hundred tons of bacon in the bacon bay, a lever exploited by the stewards. The management tried bringing in sub-contractors to move the bacon and a couple of hot heads went too far, threatening drivers and their families, and smashing a few windscreens. Many of us present did not agree with such actions even though we did not want the bacon to be moved. Unknown to many of us one of the directors was filming the action with a cine- camera, obviously to be used as evidence after the strike.

At the end of the strike we ended up with a slightly bigger pay rise than had previously been offered, I think we were all glad to be back at work. In the following weeks, one or two drivers were sacked as the film evidence went against them. Once back at work everything settled down remarkably well and work continued as before.

A new contract was acquired to ship foundry coke from Gateshead to Belfast using a special open topped thirty foot container. I was one of the first to do this job and indeed did the job many times in the future. Sometimes I went to unload scrap tin plate at West Hartlepool and then on to Gateshead, other times I just travelled empty to the Norwood coke works on the Team Valley Estate just outside Gateshead. The open topped thirty foot container was always mounted on a tri-axle skeletal trailer and the load had to be as near to twenty tons as I could manage. There was usually a big queue of local tipper drivers at the plant and it could be a long wait on some days. Before reversing with the tri-axle trailer, it was necessary to get the rear axle perfectly in line in order to drop a pin in two holes, if the axle was not straight, the pin would not go in and it meant driving forward a bit until the holes lined up. Sometimes it would take two or three shunts forward to achieve the correct position.

Once under the gantry where the coke was loaded it was a matter of guessing when you thought that the load was around twenty tons. The coke was very hot and steaming after the cooling with large quantities of water. The drivers at the plant told me that some days the coke held more water and was therefore heavier. When the plant operator, who was a better judge than I was, said it was about the right weight for my load I went round to the weighbridge. To weigh the load meant dropping the trailer on the bridge as it was too small for the complete vehicle, which was a bit of a pain. A few cwt over and the weighbridge clerk would not let me go, half a ton light meant returning to the plant to add a bit more. Anything over was thrown off by hand, taking care not get burnt fingers. The drivers waiting to load after me were very good as they usually let me nip in after a loaded tipper came out. Then it was back to the weighbridge, drop the trailer again and hope the load was correct. I think my record was three times on the bridge before the clerk and myself were satisfied. The office told me to put a sheet over the load, but as it was still very hot, I never bothered until a lot later.

If my time was up, I stayed in Gateshead a few times, parking on derelict ground, surrounded by rows of small terraced houses. I remember the young boys jumping up and hanging on the mirrors when the lorries were parking up shouting "Watch yer wagon mister". With still time to drive I would make for Brough, and then onto Kirby Stephen and the motorway at Tebay. At that time, this route was still open to heavy traffic and as I had found a good place to park, it was a perfect fiddle home. Usually one lift did it in very easily, the next morning could be a problem and I would not attempt doing that particular fiddle in winter.

It was tiring getting lifts home and sometimes I just could not be bothered, especially if the weather was bad. I think it suited Margaret and helped to create a happy medium, as I knew she did not like me being away from home most of the week.

BY SLUDGE G

With the M62 now open up to Huddersfield the journey into Yorkshire was very much easier and quicker, but at that time the traffic was nothing like today's congestion. One day a few N.I.T. drivers had loaded clay pipes at Hepworth mid-way between Sheffield and Huddersfield on the A616. It was coming into Huddersfield on this road that my beloved Borderer sustained damage. One particular roundabout in the town was at the top of a steep slope, at this roundabout we were to turn left for the motorway. A couple of other drivers were in front of me and Bert Wright was behind. As I approached the roundabout, I was trying judge the approach to try not to stop on the hill. I was about twenty yards from the top and after glancing in my offside mirror I saw Bert coming alongside me with his more powerful ERF that had the Rolls Royce engine. To my horror Bert started to cut in to the left for the turn at the roundabout, I was alongside the railings on my left and as Bert continued to come left, my cab became trapped. First Bert's trailer took my offside mirror off, and then parts of the cab, all I could was bang on the horn and flash my lights until Bert finally saw me, and stopped. Bert left his cab and it was quite funny at the time, to see him standing in the middle of the road giving me what for as I sat in my cab completely trapped. When he calmed down, he did grudgingly accept the blame for the accident. When he pulled away from the battered cab my Borderer looked a sorry sight, I was not happy man.

The lorry was just about fit to drive and when I drove into the N.I.T. yard, I just wanted to hide away. I was on the mat within ten minutes and to Bert's credit, he came in the office with me and owned up to his error. All the same, Bert was leaning over me when I filled in the accident report, we finally agreed on more toned down version and he was satisfied. It was about three weeks later when I got my Borderer back and it looked none the worse. Bert was always a good friend to me at N.I.T. and I do not think we ever spoke of it again.

Many transport digs were very good, the ones in Rotherham, Doncaster and Silvertown amongst the best, but some were really awful. The little red book that listed transport digs was only a guide; it was a bit of a lottery sometimes. My worst ever digs were near Staines, I think they were called the Aero Café. I had eaten my meal and was informed the washroom was around the back, they were very dirty and had no hot water. The beds were up above the café in the large loft space and contained over a dozen beds that lined each side. Air fresheners hung from the beams and clothes littered most of the beds, which looked unmade and scruffy. There was a commotion down stairs and then seven or eight building workers took over the small loft space. Muddy boots and clothes were thrown down, and it was pure bedlam. Another driver arrived, a Scotsman, he was very angry at the state of the place, but as he said, it was too late to move now and just make the best of it. We both went out for a drink together and on our return tried the beds but decided to sleep on top of the bedding.

Once, two of us picked some digs out of the red book when we were in Swansea, the place was nice enough but the dinner that night had been in an oven for ages and the meat was exactly like Oxo shaped cubes, the whole thing was inedible so we ate out that night. At some digs if the breakfast was particularly greasy and smelt of cheap bacon I would leave after a drink and toast, once outside I would catch a milkman on the street and drink milk until I could get a decent breakfast on my travels.

I was still delivering the bacon and it was not really a problem except in summer, when the blue- bottles and wasps swooped on the load when the sheets were removed at the drops. My boots and the bottom of my trousers went a bit crusty, but I suppose there are worse loads than the bacon. The Michelin tyre deliveries were not hard work, but I found them boring and standing in a forty foot container bowling thousands of mini tyres out one at a time was not something I liked doing. Much of the Michelin work centred on Stoke depot, a place I tried to avoid if possible. When having to call at Stoke for fuel was unavoidable, it was best to be in and out as quickly as possible. Depending on the time of day, they could keep you over-night to load another trailer the next day. Some of their work was from Stanton and Stavely near Derby and consisted of cast pipes and other cast metalwork. It was an easy enough load but took forever, being stuck in their huge stockyard made the hours really drag.

The small depot at Frampton Cotterell was another N.I.T. depot that I visited a number of times when delivering in the area. I remember going to the old Fry's chocolate factory at Keynsham and delivering bacon in the Bath and Bristol area. It was usually only a flying visit to this depot and they did not keep us there unlike London or Stoke.

When in Bristol I stayed once or twice at digs in Midland Road but never liked them as I thought they were noisy and scruffy. I found a better place to stay at the city centre end of Coronation Road, which was a very homely place run by an elderly woman. It was far better than the dump on Midland Road. Parking at Coronation Road was a problem and meant going to the other side of the river onto Cumberland Road, it was only a short walk back over the bridge to the digs. I came out of these digs one morning to find someone had pinched both my mirror glasses, the rubbers where still attached, so I thought it probably wasn't kids but another driver. Driving with no mirrors felt like I was driving blind, exaggerating the distance required when turning, and unable to see anything down the sides. After a lot of messing around, I managed to find a place that had the correct size mirrors; it felt a lot better with them fitted.

Another small depot was in Cardiff, it was not a depot as such, more of an office. It was located around or on the Bute Street area, a very famous area of Cardiff with a touch of notoriety, Tiger Bay. We had a few good nights around there and I remember being there with Bert Wright and three or four other N.I.T.drivers, we went to some very strange places that night. We went in one pub and most of the women looked, and were dressed like men, we did not stay long there. Another pub was full of a certain type of woman, some rough but some were not bad lookers. After a great night out, we all got chips and walked back to the digs. At that time in the early seventies most large cities had a certain area that many people only ever read about in the News of the World.

At Preston, where the regime was a bit strict the management kept a tight hold on the drivers. We used to hang around at the services on the M61 near Preston and the manager spied on us at these services. Going out again in the late afternoon did not appeal to everyone and some had dodges to avoid this happening. The strokes pulled included complaining about a mysterious fault on their unit or pulling a couple of wires out of the trailer lights, a dodge soon found by the fitters, but it all took time. Once it got to a certain time they could refuse to go out again that day, sometimes it worked and other times it did not.

Margaret and I were not getting on to well and it was probably my fault. I know that I could be moody for no reason, and did not get on with Margaret's family, but sometimes when I had been away for two or three days, or had a fiddle home and it was late, I did wonder what the point of it all was. There seemed to be no happy medium between home and work, okay I was a bit of a workaholic but I was certainly a good provider. My being away was not something Margaret liked, it came to a head after a big row, things were said, and typical of me I said without thinking that I would get a local job. N.I.T. had no local drivers but I was confident that local work was out there. I jumped the gun somewhat by giving my notice in and it was not until mid-week that Bernard a mate at N.I.T. said to try WH Malcolm's as his son was in the traffic office there. On the Friday, I had been to Teeside with a tank to collect Formaldehyde and on my way to the docks; I drove into Malcolm's yard at Lostock Hall. It was quite simple really, a few questions, a small form to fill in and there it was, start on Monday. Talk about luck, but that was cutting it a bit fine to say the least.

CHAPTER FOUR
THE SCOTTISH CONNECTION

My first day at Malcolms was quite an easy introduction to my new job. I was to drive an Atkinson Mk 2, with the 180 Gardner, which was clean and tidy as were all Malcolm's vehicles. My first delivery was a load of forty foot steel angles to a steel stockholder in Smethwick, the load; being chained and unsheeted was an easy start for me. It was dinnertime before I was unloaded and after my break, I rang Preston and Harry told me to go to the Heinz factory at Kitt Green. At the factory, I met the Heinz shunter, a man called John who was to be a good mate for many years.

John's job was to load and sheet the WH Malcolm's trailers, he explained that some days he needed help if there were too many loads for him to handle. I stayed helping John for most of the afternoon and at break time we went to the canteen and over a brew, John filled me in on everything about the work, the drivers, and the office staff at Preston depot. The work came down at night from Glasgow and the loads were mainly all types of steel including plate, angles, flats and coils along with whisky, structural steelwork, bottles, and from Chryslers at Linwood came car parts going to Chryslers at Stoke Works near Coventry. All this made up a lot of the varied loads coming south. At the depot, there were about a dozen drivers, two on night trunk, about five on shunting and the rest distance drivers. Bob the manager was a big Scotsman in his late fifties with a very easy attitude to the drivers. If you did your job as required, the drivers would be trusted, things were un-regimented unlike N.I.T. where it was a bit strong. Bob's assistant in the office was Harry, John said he watched P.N.E. and I thought that was a good start. The one thing John told me was that there was always plenty of overtime. Six am starts were the norm and Saturday work was always available. In addition there was work in the yard in an evening, transhipping, making loads up, and generally getting the trunk loads ready for five or six Scottish trunk drivers who came 5 nights a week. All the units were Atkinson's and all were 180 Gardner's apart from one, the Preston depot tended to get the hand-me-downs from Scotland. A mileage bonus paid to drivers going outside a 50-mile radius amounted to three and half pence per mile on anything above 25mph. Therefore, a Birmingham done in two hours was about £1.75 each way, and as John said, it was all money on top of the overtime. It was good to get all this information about Malcolms from John who struck me as a man who would go out of his way to help you.

After our longish afternoon break, John told me to ring the office to see if I was to take any loads back to Preston. On ringing, Harry told me to bring a load back to the yard and then return to Heinz for another. When I returned to Heinz, I met a couple of the other shunters and together we finished roping and fly sheeting the remaining trailers. We all returned to the depot and after fuelling up Bob told us that there was a bit of work to do in the yard, it was mainly filling spaces on a couple of loaded trailers with any extra pallets or cases off other part loads. By this time, it was approaching 7 o'clock and as everyone waited for the hour to come up on the time clock, I did the same.

Driving the short distance home, I was thinking that over 4 hours overtime with over £3 or so in bonus was a good wage for the day.

During the next few weeks I met all the other drivers who were mostly around my age except for a couple who were in their forties. All seemed good blokes and their company was entertaining and relaxed. Alan, who lived not far from me, became another good mate; he told me that John was the first drivers to start at Malcolms. He said John was the self-appointed foreman but everyone accepted this as John's wholehearted way of working. Alan was a man who only worked one speed, which was slow. As I tended to be highly active we were opposites in our work ethic, but we got along and that was the main thing. John had nicknamed Alan as "Concorde," later Alan was to name me "Itchy feet" as he said I could not keep still. Apart from the Heinz work, Malcolms loaded bottles at Knottingley, oil from Texaco Trafford Park, and many other smaller contracts. WH Malcolm in the early seventies was one of the largest haulage contractors in the West of Scotland with depots in Johnstone, Glasgow, Paisley and Killwinning on the Ayrshire Coast. The regime was a bit stricter north of the border and the Scottish drivers thought we had it easy at Preston. All the Glasgow drivers were great blokes to meet and many of them had a wicked sense of humour, many a time they gave the English some stick, sheep were mentioned along with Hadrian's Wall.

Gradually as the weeks went by two new drivers started and I was no longer the last man in, which made me feel more secure. Not that there was any job insecurity for anyone as Malcolms were getting busier all the time. I was still in touch with Freddie and Bob from N.I.T. and we saw each other at the football, but I had a new set of workmates, everyone moves on and things change all the time.

As I said, most drivers had to do work in an evening making loads up for the trunks. Some drivers and I include myself, grabbed all the overtime that was available, but if you cannot do long hours in the transport industry, you are in the wrong job, and if you cannot do this when you are young there is no hope for you later in life. That has always been my philosophy and it worked for me. One particular night Bob told us to move a milk tank to a different trailer; the tank was about ten foot by five foot, stainless steel and glass lined. Andy who was driving the fork truck (his bad luck) lifted one end of the tank, and one of us put some timber under so that Andy could get the forks right under. He lifted it off the trailer and was moving across the yard with his forks near the ground. As he neared the other trailer he slowly lifted the forks but unfortunately, as he did this a front wheel of the fork truck went into a large hole in the concrete. The tank slid off the forks like butter from a hot knife and crashed to the ground. It was obvious that the tank was badly dented but we were not sure about the glass lining. Andy went as white as a sheet, and jumped off the fork truck shouting that he was not driving it again. Harry told us to put on the trailer; it was to go north all the same. We believe the phone lines from Glasgow to Preston the next day were red hot as the damage was found. It was an unfortunate accident and not something we wanted to repeat.

Many exports came down on the trunks and sometimes two or three of us were on the same job at Liverpool docks. In the seventies Liverpool docks was still a very busy place as containerisation, though growing was nowhere near as huge as it is today. The queues could be very long, stretching down the dock road from the gates at the many docks. Booking in took forever, stood in the rain with dozens of other drivers, and that was only the start. Not long after booking in it was break time and we usually went to the dockers canteens, which were really surprisingly good for the price. After the break it was just a matter of keep moving up with the queue until you eventually at least got through the gate. This felt better as you more or less knew you were not far from being tipped. Handball jobs were taken into the sheds, the foreman giving us an area to unload our trailers. Whisky was unloaded into a secure fenced area with the customs checking everything. A docker was not allowed onto the trailer and once a space was cleared on the deck, empty pallets were lifted on and it was up to us to stack the pallets. Every case of whisky had to have its shipping marks showing on the outside and the pallet was stacked with a hollow down the middle to achieve this. A gang of dockers was always with you but did no work, just watched us sweating which got annoying sometimes.

Another regular job that came from Glasgow was large packing cases of bathroom suites, wash-basins, bidets and toilets, packed two or three of each in slatted cases made of rough-cut timber. They were all destined for the Middle East and tens of thousands were sent there, it makes you think what they had been using in the past. The cases were pigs to unload as they had to be stacked on pallets or on the shed floor and three washbasins in a wooden case were extremely heavy. Most of the time there would be two or three Malcolm drivers together so it made the job a bit easier. Still the Arabs must have had a few cracked fittings to glue together, especially when a slat broke off the case when being lifted and it fell to the ground, the packing cases were very shoddy really. All in all the dock deliveries gave us time to chat and clean the cab as well as taking it easy for a while at least. As far as deliveries to factories and warehouses were concerned, many treated lorry drivers with indifference. On arrival at these drops you could be greeted with a variety of greetings, too late, dinnertime or you have a long wait. In bad weather, the sheets could not be taken off and when it was your time to unload, they would watch you wrapping the sheets up from the warehouse door. At these places it was best not to say anything because at some time you would be visiting them again.

The management at Malcolms did not mind drivers swapping jobs, either from shunting to trunk or distance; it did not matter as long as someone was willing to swap as well. John had decided he wanted to come out of Heinz and become a shunter; he was now self-appointed road foreman, a born organizer who got things moving. John was well known for having a stock of girlie magazines in his cab and did swaps at different places. One evening before we went home Concorde put a girly magazine in John's bag that he carried his flask and sandwiches in, Concorde zipped the bag up and John had no idea what was in store for him. It just had to happen; John's wife was sorting the bag out for the next day and found the magazine; John had to think very quickly. The next day he knew exactly who the culprit was and Concorde was suitably sworn at.

Things were running pretty smoothly at home, but I still often had a strong feeling of restlessness, especially at weekends when I did feel rather trapped. However, there was harmony so I subdued the feelings for now. Apart from Margaret's parents always there, I now had to contend with her sister's new husband who was a white-collar worker on the railway. We had nothing in common,

I thought he was a young man who knew everything, but had done nothing.

Malcolms were expanding and an opportunity to go on trunk arose when a driver fancied a change and try shunting. We spoke to Bob and he agreed to let us swap the following week. Preston still only had the Atkinsons and over four hundred miles a night was a push with the 180 Gardners especially as most loads were full weight. My running mate was Rick a driver who had come from W-J Ridings just after I started. The trunk drivers at Preston worked on a week about basis, that is to say, there were two drivers to the unit, one did a week of nights, and the other shunted the same unit on days, the next week we swapped and so it went on. It took a bit of getting used to as the system upset your body clock, so weekends was a difficult time to sleep properly. Although the official starting time for the trunkers was around 7pm, we all agreed to have everything ready for six thirty at night. My mate on the unit was Smithy, a Leyland bloke about my age; I was pleased that we were already friends as a good working relationship was important.

Monday nights proved to be the worst of the week for feeling tired, after sleeping normally on the Sunday and being up during the day, the early hours of Tuesday were particularly difficult. Some people cannot adjust to this way of working; one driver had to stop doing it as it was making him ill. The next few weeks were very tiring, on the return journeys I was sticking my head out of the window to freshen myself up. At first we usually did Preston to Johnstone non-stop, have our break there, and then another break on the return leg at the Moss Café at Carlisle, usually staying for forty five minutes or so.

The M6 to Carlisle was straightforward but the A74 had a 40mph speed limit and at that time was not a very wide carriageway, but was in the process of being widened by a couple of feet in places. The M8 and the Monkland motorway was a way off being completed, so after coming off the M74 where it ended at the Zoo, the route was through the City down London road past Celtic FC and onto the A8 near Rangers FC.

After that it was a short hop onto the top end of the M8, past the airport and off the motorway, passing the car plant at Linwood on the left and on into Johnstone. On arrival at Johnstone, the watchman Davy would open the gates to let us in; we then fuelled up before changing trailers. The loaded trailers were usually well sheeted and roped, but as was my usual practice, I liked to put another rope on here and there and generally tighten things up. Steel loads usually had chains already on, if they hadn't, we carried chains and dwangs with us. If the load was angled steel, we levered the top layer tight together as they tended to walk out towards the back of the trailer. All this extra checking and securing was something I had into the habit of doing, not just for road safety but also for peace of mind. There is nothing worse than driving, especially in the dark, wondering if your load is secure on the trailer. If the steel loads were already chained we had to leave our chains in the yard, but sometimes I would use an extra chain and only leave one at Johnstone. The next night at Preston the first thing said to me was that I had not left enough chains at Johnstone, but I still always used an extra chain if I thought the load needed it.

Rick and I quickly reached a good understanding with each other and it worked very well for us. Whoever had the heaviest load was in front, the other with a lighter load always stayed behind. A couple of flashes of the nearside indicator would bring the other alongside and with the cab light on and a bit of sign language we could get a message across. Whether it was stopping for a leak or if we were getting chips that night, it was a good way of communicating. It was always a good way to check the loads, lights and tyres without stopping. In the first couple of months, we both had tyre blowouts, both when carrying steel coils. They were loaded on purpose built coil carriers but the loaders always placed a fifteen ton coil to far back on the trailer, the lighter coil was usually ok near the front. This was not good for trailer tyres, which tended to be remoulds or even retreads, apart from that it was also not good for traction in bad weather. A tyre about to blow throws off a lot of smoke which looks worse in the headlights of anything following, but we would not go near them in that condition, let them blow first and then stop and do the change, especially as a lot of wheels still had the old locking rings fitted. We could change a wheel in twenty minutes or so depending if the wheel nuts were not seized, but with a length of scaffolding tube and both of us jumping on it, we could manage it. Getting the spare wheel off the unit was a pain in wet weather and we usually threw the blown wheel and tyre onto a bit of space on the trailer. This justified running together all the time, and as far as wheel changing was concerned two pairs of hands were better than one.

The 40mph speed limit on the A74 was usually upped to fifty (or more) by many night drivers but you had to keep watch all the time, we got to know where the police usually hid and received warnings from drivers approaching. The police coming from behind were a nuisance, so anything coming from behind and it was best to slow down until they passed, if it was the police they could follow for a while, then shoot past and hide in the distance. In winter, it was a lot easier as after midnight there were very few cars on the road. The police also had the habit of parking with their headlights shining across the road and as they knew who was on the road every night, any strangers would be followed and stopped.

Sometimes we got a visit from the "Big Man" Donald Malcolm, the watchman was in radio contact with Donald Malcolm and he would call Davy and ask if the Preston trunks were in, if we were, he told Davy to be at the gates to let him in. Sweeping into the depot in his big Mercedes he would drive down the yard past all his lorries parked in a long line and then come to the office. Donald Malcolm was a big man and was owner of a very large company, but he was a man who you could talk to. When he talked to us, there was always a smile on his face and a twinkle in his eyes. Usually the first thing he looked at would be the diesel sheet and anything over thirty gallons would bring the comment about the size of our boots. Sometimes he would have a couple of sips of coffee from our flasks and generally, it was very relaxed. When it was time to leave, he would walk to our lorries with us and after giving us a cigar; wish us a safe journey home. He was one of the nicest bosses anyone could wish to meet, a great man.

PHOTO COURTESY OF GYLES CARPENTER

Our weeks shunting were going well as far as overtime and mileage bonus was concerned, especially with steel to the Midlands and the Chrysler parts to Coventry, we got decent runs nearly everyday. Usually from the Midlands, it was back to the Heinz factory to help there. Tipping in Yorkshire nearly always meant loading bottles at Knottingley or Doncaster. Bottles of every shape and size were made at these works, even tiny little scent bottles which were a good load as the density of the glass meant the load was single pallet high. Doncaster had a huge stockyard that contained millions of bottles on pallet stacks. Glass milk bottles were still in use then and we did many loads of these and at two pallets high, it was very nearly a full weight load. We usually had the big bottle sheets with us and that made it a lot easier, if we only had the small sheets it took more time but still looked well. Everyone at Malcolms took a pride in the sheeting and roping, there is nothing worse than an untidy load with flapping sheets.

When on nights, Rick, who was a bit of a ladies man, sometimes would disappear up a slip road of a major junction, over the roundabout and rejoin the motorway, looking for skirt as he called it. Leaving either depot Rick made sure he was first to the motorway to have a chance of picking someone up, female that is, males were treated to a blast of spray or dust. Coming out of Glasgow on London Road if he saw any other lorries approaching the lights along Tollcross Road he was away like James Hunt, he had to be there first. In the dark Rick would stop for any female but odd times he ended up with an old boot, who was deposited at the next café, he had some taste.

We had been on nights for around six months with the Atkinson 180 Gardners, we both on odd occasions used the only Atkinson left that had a 150 Gardner, and that was a real struggle considering the distance we had to do. However we were to get new units at last, not a Volvo 88 or a Scania as the Glasgow trunkers had, but to me anyway, units that I had a liking for, the Atkinson Borderer with 220 Cummins engine and Fuller gearbox. We both got our new units on the same night, they were both hooked up and ready when we arrived at Johnstone. We ran them in for the rest of the week, but even taking it easy, the difference from the old Atkinsons was chalk and cheese. The 220 Cummins engine, while small by today's standards was a very gutsy engine and did not give up on the hills as our old units did. The Cummins engine and the Fuller gearbox complimented each other and sounded great when pulling and going through the gears. It also made a change to have a cab that did not rattle, was draught free and had a heater that worked.

With the coming of the new units, I became even more of a stickler for cab cleanliness. When on days I would black and polish the interior, even polishing the floor. Smithy was a smoker as I was, but he was a messy smoker, leaving ash all over. Still it was easily cleaned up and as we both got on together, it was nothing really.

A new driver started on days, and he was yet another Jack, he had come from Woodside's who did change overs in Preston. We both struck up an immediate friendship that in the future was to lead to trouble at home for us both. Malcolms were getting more new work all the time and there was a big increase in the loads out of H J Heinz. We were now getting loads for the south from Heinz as before all loads were for Scotland. We were also loading steel slabs at Scunthorpe, Volvo cabs at Immingham, concrete segments in Yorkshire and many other varied jobs that general haulage entails. The new power station at Drax was being constructed and many loads of steelwork were coming down from Scotland, this work along with loads for a power station at Isle of Grain near Rochester, which was to start in 1975 was very good for us at Preston. The power station work was made up of pipe work, large parts for the boilers and structural steelwork. The Scottish drivers on distance work did all the wide loads, along with the long loads on trombone trailers, so the loads coming on trunk where the normal loads on forty foot and fifty foot trailers. Babcock Power the makers of all this steelwork had a huge stockyard complete with overhead cranes on the massive site at Drax. All the loads were unloaded in this stockyard until needed on the actual construction site. It was a good day out, unloading at Drax and then maybe loading bottles at Doncaster, overtime and mileage bonus, a good combination.

I had been at Malcolm's over two years and was continuing with the trunk one week, and days the next, with no adverse effect. Rick and I had one or two difficult nights but overall everything went smoothly, in fact I think we both quite enjoyed being on trunk. We sort of got to know a lot of the other trunkers even if we did not speak to them. In summer, we recognized many trucks coming towards us and we usually waved or flashed the lights. Even in winter it was possible to spot most of them by the cab top lights or illuminated name, they were nearly all different from a distance. Going north and approaching the Barrow in Furness junction, it was uncanny how many times the Bowater trunk from Barrow was joining the motorway as we approached. We would fly past them waving like mad, but they had always caught us up as we went up Shap as their loads were only toilet rolls. However, going down to Penrith we shot past them giving them the wanker sign. John Kirby who drove for Latham's car transporters at Preston was another mate at night; we would meet at the Moss café on the way back, along with many other regulars we got to know. John from Lathams had an Atkinson rigid and trailer, his Atki had a 240 Gardner and could pass us easily , but he did suffer when it was windy and he was loaded with cars going to Bathgate, John was lucky as he returned empty all the time. On clear nights, especially in winter when it was frosty, you could see across all the fields and even spot foxes sometimes, but it was the wind in winter that got us down a bit. No matter which way you were going it was impossible to escape its clutches. After leaving Preston and on the M6 heading north to Forton you got an idea of what it was going to be like and that the diesel figures would be up. Further north it was like hitting a brick wall, at slight inclines where we usually made it over without dropping a gear, it was now necessary to do just that, still there was always the Moss café to look forward to on the return. The Moss was a bit of a dive and I would never eat anything there but at least the tea was boiled. If the ferry had docked at Stranraer, the lorry park could be full of Irish drivers along with the mainland drivers. Sometimes it was a problem parking when it was busy and a queue could build up on the entrance. If the Police came by when this happened they waved us on, once even shouting that our next café was Southwaite Services. We knew another trunker who worked for Archbold from Leeds; his arms were so covered with tattoos that it was hard to see any clear skin. He was a good laugh and was always goading Fred about our Atkinson's. He drove an ERF, and said it only had a 220 Cummins the same as ours, but he always passed us easily when obviously fully loaded. Rick swore that he had a 250 Cummins and it got up Rick's nose a bit. It was easily solved by having a look at the ERF but we never did, truth known, Rick would rather it be a 250 and then there was no reflection on his ability to get the best out of the 220 Cummins. In the summer months and heading south, we would see the Scottish Motor Traction coaches all heading south full of holidaymakers. Some of the coaches were quite old and we could usually pass them, sometimes even on the hills. The younger passengers that were not asleep would always give us a wave as we passed each other, it all helped to relieve the boredom a bit. There was a time when a bakers strike was taking place in England and bread was very scarce. Coming out of Glasgow I remember stopping at a shop run by an Indian man, it was after mid-night and he was still open, I bought about ten loaves and soon sold them on the next day, I repeated this a few times until the strike ended.

Jack Sugden a distance driver got the first MAN 232 sleeper cab at Preston depot and when we looked inside it did make the Atkinson cab look very dated. The MAN had; double bunks, blinds, storage space, a walk through cab and a luxury item--a radio. The column gear change was a very strange and Jack said it was difficult at first. We were to use this unit on odd nights and found it nice to drive but useless on hills, the Cummins 220 was a far better engine, as was the Fuller gearbox. The MAN had no guts at all and just seemed to give up in the wind and on the steeper hills.

The other Jack who had started from Woodsides sometime ago, asked me if I fancied a night out and before long we had started to go out on a Friday night every other week. It was not going down very well in either household, Margaret accusing Jack of leading me astray and Jacks wife saying something along the same lines. At first it was quite tame just going for a couple of drinks but developed into going clubbing fully suited up. We were getting home in the small hours of Saturday morning, but we were having such good nights that it did not bother us, I think we both felt as free as birds. Both of us had married at a very young age, twenty for me and nineteen for Jack and we both thought that we had missed out somehow. Sally and David my children were lovely kids and being brought up wonderfully by Margaret but I still had this restless feeling and the thought of freedom to do what I wanted, when I wanted, persisted.

Rick and I had a run in with the police one night when heading north and we could not have chosen a worse officer to tangle with. It was a calm, frosty and clear night; we had just come over Beatock and were speeding downhill on a clear road towards the bends at Elvanfoot when I saw by the light of a full moon, the police landrover in front. I slowed right down, Rick who had also seen him opened up a bigger gap between us. Hoping he was going to turn off at Crawford or Abingdon, we sat it out at just below forty mph. He did not turn off but continued on past Cairn Lodge and towards Lesmahagow where the road was lit. It seemed as if he was playing a game because he kept slowing right down to thirty odd miles an hour, then speeding up when we drew near. Going around the bends in Lesmahagow and onto the straight before the motorway I decided that at forty mph I was entitled to pass him. This was just what he had been waiting for, as I drew near in the outside lane, four fingers were stuck out of his window. He then straddled the white line, put his blue light and stop sign on and forced us to a halt. As he walked back to us Rick and I were out of our cabs and we saw he was a sergeant, probably the sergeant we had heard about. I got the first words in by asking what was going on, he snapped back that if his speedo showed forty mph and I passed him he would book me. After having a rant about speeding lorry drivers and warning us, he finished with the comment about being "After you Malcolm's drivers". It turned out he was the sergeant who had a hatred of lorries and lorry drivers in general.

Upgrading was taking place on parts of the A74, mainly to make the carriageways a bit wider. It felt narrow especially when passing another lorry in the rain and wind and care was needed. The road works meant crossing the central reservation to the other carriageway that was coned off. At new works, it was best to slow right down to see what the camber was like, and after that had been judged and depending on your load, it was possible to cross over at a reasonable speed. If when you were crossing and just at that time, another lorry was hammering towards you it was a bit nervy at that critical moment. On the whole, we hardly saw any accidents on the A74 at night in winter, the summer months did bring some accidents though, mainly involving cars and caravans.

This brings me nicely to Rick's, mine and a certain Mr. Clarkson's pet hate, caravans and stupid caravaners. On Friday nights in summer when we joined the motorway at Bamber Bridge, all we could see was two solid lanes of caravans. It was impossible to get above forty mph and even when gaps appeared in the inside lane they all continued in the middle lane. When the motorway cleared a bit around Lancaster, they were still under our feet. Three or four caravans could be going along quite nicely as you approached to pass them, when the middle one decided to be leader for a bit and with two or three flashes on the indicator he was out, usually at the bottom of a hill, leaving us slowing down in the middle lane. Going down the hills, some were still determined to pass even if we were already past fifty five mph, after slowing a bit to let them go, they passed at over sixty mph, waddling all over and the drivers wife sat with the AA maps on her knee. Invariably they slowed to fifty mph after passing and forcing us to pass them yet again. Some travelled half the night, probably after the driver had been at work all day and nothing to stop him doing so. Parking overnight in a lay-by on the A74 is not my idea of a holiday; they must have spilt their tea when a speeding lorry blasted past their lay-by. Rick and I sometimes stopped at Southwaite services for a quick cup of tea and in summer the queues were always long, so doing what we usually did, we walked to the front to get our tea. A cry went up about queue jumping and a supervisor came up and told us to wait our turn in the queue of trippers getting meals. Explaining that we were lorry drivers and only wanted tea did no good, so rather than wait Rick said, "Stuff you tea" and I finished it off by saying they were glad of our custom in winter.

PHOTO COURTESY OF GYLES CARPENTER

After the Southwaite episode, Rick suggested stopping at the Little Chef at Gretna that allowed lorries at the time. The Little Chef was a motel as well as a café, to get to the café meant walking past the motel reception where a young woman was on duty. After a few visits, we were saying hello to each other and Rick who had the gift of chatting women up began to linger at the reception, talking to the receptionist like an old friend. It was happening every night and in the end I would leave him at Gretna and carry on, it broke our understanding but there was no choice really, and it was to lead to Rick's downfall later.

It all started when Rick got a new unit, a Volvo F88, I was told that I would also get an F88 in a couple of months. So for the next seven or eight weeks it was to be the tortoise and the hare. We still stopped at Gretna, but Rick felt he could spend more time there as he now had the Volvo and could make up the lost time. He complained following me in my Borderer was not doing his fuel figures any good and that he was not getting the best out of his Volvo. His stays at Gretna grew longer until in the end Rick was hammering the Volvo to catch up. Mostly I was running on my own now, sometimes hardly seeing Rick at all. Towards the middle of the second month I saw some new units being prepared at Johnstone, a couple of 88's and two Mercedes 1924, I had a good look at the Volvo's and thought to that it would not be long now before I got one of them. It was quite a shock to find out that I was to get one of the Mercedes units. When I asked about this at Preston, Bob said that Johnstone were not sending Volvo F88's to Preston to get hammered. There was nothing I could except to have a go at Rick for putting his love life before his job and spoiling it for others. The Volvo F88 was to be the only one that was ever sent to Preston depot, even though we did get Scanias later.

JIM McLAREN JNR. IN 1975
PHOTO COURTESY OF JIM McLAREN JNR.

The Mercedes 1924 was to be the worst unit I ever drove, it was supposed to be rated at 235 HP, but where these horses had got to I don't know, maybe still on the continent. It just would not pull at all, it gave up on hills, and the brakes were pretty awful. The gear stick was too far to the left and gave me a pain in my side when changing gear, which was often. I would have willingly kept my Borderer, which was a far better unit on many counts. As there were no other 1924's on the road at night it was a bit of a novelty for a while, later many friends took great delight in passing me on the hills. Rick continued with his courting every other week and I plodded on with my useless Mercedes, making the best of a disappointing episode that could have worked out if the Little Chef had not been visited. On one of the nights when I was heading south on my own I stopped on a lay-by at the top of Beatock. It was a regular stop either to have a leak or to check the load and trailer and as usual I walked around the back of the trailer on the offside, and came back up the other. It was a particularly dark night and as I stood by the unit doing what you do, I had a feeling that someone had walked past me. I couldn't see anyone, but it did spook me a bit and I dived into the cab. As I set off there was nothing to be seen in the headlights but I still thought someone or something had passed me in the dark. I did stop at the lay-by again but never felt comfortable at that spot. Smithy my mate on the Mercedes came off nights to go on distance work. He was given a Bedford TM, a bit of a strange unit for Malcolms, it was to be the only one I ever saw on the fleet. Lawrence, a very quiet man was to become my new partner. Lawrence was one of those people who somehow didn't look or act like a lorry driver, he looked more like an office worker, but he did the job and that was what mattered I suppose.

My own problems came to a head after a particularly late night out with Jack, I think the writing was on the wall for my marriage as well as Jack's and certainly Rick's. It was really the fact that I wanted my freedom back, and saw the prospect of continuing with this feeling not something I wanted to do. Margaret and I finally split up and I went to live in Preston at my sister Joanne's house. A while later I attended the courts and was ordered to pay maintenance every week, it was quite a large amount but was manageable and I accepted that I had to pay for my families upkeep. Hindsight is supposed to be a wonderful thing and a few years later I regretted my actions, especially not seeing the children growing up. It is easy to say but I honestly believe that if Margaret and I could have got through the next five years or so, then everything would have turned out better. However, "What is done is done" as they say, Margaret kept the house and everything in it, and had a reasonable amount of money, and dare I say it, she had her mother, who would be on her side and help her tremendously.

JIM McLAREN SNR. AND HIS NEW DAF 3300
PHOTO COURTESY OF JIM McLAREN JNR.

The depot at Preston was by now getting rather full, more and more trailers were squeezed into the small yard making it difficult parking up. Late on Friday afternoon was the worst time, all the Preston drivers returning, Scottish driver calling for fuel and some of us trying to some transhipping job in the middle of it all. The narrow road over the two bridges at the entrance to the depot was sometimes at a standstill with a queue of Malcolm's lorries waiting to enter. Once in the yard, it was so full it made turning round or the parking of trailers very difficult. An hours overtime could be gained just waiting to fuel up or park a trailer. It was very frustrating waiting to start a transhipping job as every space was filled, the top and bottom of it was that the depot was now just too small. Along the right hand side of the yard a row of houses had been built, separated from the depot by small gardens and a wire fence. The noise must have been annoying, even more so when the Glasgow trunks arrived around midnight. Early the next morning Preston trunks would be returning and early starters leaving which left the people in the house very little quite time. Still the depot was open before the houses were built, so they all knew what was at the bottom of their gardens when they moved in. Getting out of the depot was a bit tight especially with a fifty foot trailer, the lady who lived in a bungalow opposite stood in her window trying to catch any driver who ran on her kerb. The council eventually erected a small metal barrier in front of her property; I think just to stop her moaning and complaining to the Town Hall.

Derek, a Preston driver who was only about five foot three inches tall had been nicknamed as Smurf, even though he was an explosive character he took his new name very well. In the corner of the yard there was a very large concrete sewer pipe, about eight foot long and five foot high. Concorde had somewhere found a child's toy dog, the one that could be pushed around on wheels; it was quite big dog and looked very realistic. Concorde put the dog at the far end of the pipe and put it around that a stray dog was living in the yard, hoping to trick Smurf. A while later John asked Smurf if he had any food left for the dog, he added that the dog was back in the pipe so off Smurf went to get some food. By now, it was going dark and the sight of Smurf trying to coax the toy dog out of the pipe and being watched by us all was something very hilarious, it could have been on television.

More and better work was passing through Preston depot as the months flew past; some of it was work we had never handled before. The heavy haulage company West of Scotland did a lot of work for Terex the heavy plant equipment manufacturers. Huge dump trucks for the opencast coalmines were transported south by West of Scotland, all minus the wheels and some of the cab parts.

The wheels and other parts were all delivered by Malcolms to the mines were a team of engineers would fit the dump trucks together. We also did work for British Crane Hire, moving jib and tower sections along with the ballast weights from Morley near Leeds. Structural steelwork for general building sites came down to us at Preston for delivery in Lancashire and Yorkshire. A particular job that could be straightforward or a lot of hard work came from Kilwinning at night. The loads were white granules of a chemical; it was in shiny, slippery bags stacked on pallets and were destined for the Nobel's factory at Penrhyndeudraeth. Almost every time these loads came on trunk, they had slipped into the sheets, and to be met by a slipped load of these bags at 5am was not good. The loads usually came two at a time and usually one of them had slipped. Taking the sheets off and hoping even more bags didn't fall off was hard work first thing in a morning and took over an hour to sort out. These loads apart, it all made the job more interesting and obviously a lot busier. The Heinz factory at Kitt Green was still the main source of work and the volume of loads had increased tremendously over the past two years. W.J.Riding had a shunter at the factory along with Gaskells but many other local companies large and small relied on Heinz for their work. All the fork-truck drivers were always very helpful especially with regard to getting the sheets onto the top of the load. The best thing by far was the canteen, the meals were excellent and although we paid a bit more than Heinz employees it was still extremely cheap. The canteen was a bit segregated with the office staff in the so called posh part, all drivers usually all being together in one area, but it must have been one of the best canteens in the country. Sometimes, when there were a lot of trailers to load, one of us would be at the factory all day helping the shunter, this meant we could have regular breaks during the day, not something a lorry driver can always manage.

PHOTO COURTESY OF JIM McLAREN JNR.

Rick and I continued on trunk until Rick decided that the new love in his life was living too far away. He had split from his wife who had left the family house, giving Rick the chance to bring his new girlfriend back to Preston to live with him. Rick came off nights and went on distance work but it never really suited him as being in love he wanted to be home, sometimes he would take his girlfriend with him, mainly to keep an eye on her, as she was quite a stunner. It was not much later when Rick was sacked for doing a flyer home from Motherwell one night when his time was up, he was unlucky enough to be stopped by the police for something unrelated and got found out. John fancied another change so decided to take Rick's place on trunk. John kept the Volvo for the time being and to give him credit we slotted back into the earlier system that Rick and I had used. He stayed behind the entire time, got a bit close sometimes and bobbed around behind me but a little touch on the brakes to show the brake lights and he usually got the message. As I said before John was a bit bossy and even on nights he was no different. "You start putting the chains on" or "give us a hand here", but it was just his way and never bothered me, I usually ignored him. When going through Glasgow it was as though John didn't know the way, as he kept tight behind me, even through traffic lights that I just managed to get over on the change. However, on the dual carriageway passing Linwood he was past and gone, to be first at the pumps.

Margaret and I were now legally separated and I saw the children, probably not as often as I should have done, yet another of my regrets. Jack and I were still going out every other week and even though Jack was married and living at home we both acted as single men. I was seeing someone else, a girl called Ann who was a switchboard operator. She came with me on trunk a few times on Friday nights but was a bit of a nuisance, as she kept wanting to go to the ladies, not easy on the A74 at night. One particular night at Johnstone, Donald Malcolm paid one of his customary visits. Spotting Ann in the cab, he climbed in and had a good chat to her and then told me to look after the young lady. Some company bosses would have raised the roof about carrying passengers but that was not the Donald Malcolm way. Ann and I had a holiday together in Ibiza were I was expected to spend what money I had on everything, Ann paid for nothing and it got up my nose quite a lot. On our return the talk was getting round to the future and I did not want to discuss things like that, I felt that it was ok for now, but certainly not serious enough to start talking of getting engaged.

After the holiday and back at work on days, I heard Jack had been in a bit of bother. He had thrown a small machine off on a roundabout near Coventry, as it was not his first escapade he was put in Heinz as a punishment. The work in Heinz was heavy, boring and uncomfortable in bad weather and was not helped by inconsiderate drivers, there was nothing worse than finding sheets that had been folded inside out. At busy times, drivers were sent to Heinz to help, some hated it but others including myself thought it made a change. The loading bays at the factory were under cover but it was a bit tight reversing in on the blind side until you had got used to it. We all used to stand there watching a stranger trying to reverse into a bay , sometimes seven or eight shunts and he was still not in the right place. There is nothing worse than being watched and this usually made some make an even bigger mess of it, marks out of ten were usually awarded on completion. Accidents did happen at the factory, most involving the drivers, some of which were comical in a strange sort of way. Pulling out from under a loaded and unsheeted trailer before winding the legs down was one I saw a couple of times, you would not believe the mess of cans and cartons it made. Another driver drove off the weighbridge and was too sharp on the clutch and the back pallets split and blocked the bridge. Yet another left the weighbridge with an unsheeted load and turned to sharply to the right and the trailer wheels hit a stubby concrete bollard, this threw half the load off. The reason for going on the weighbridge before sheeting up was that if the weight did not tally with the notes, a checker had to come to find the discrepancy. Many a stranger had made a lovely job of sheeting and roping only to find that his weight was out. It must have been very annoying to have to take all the ropes and sheets off to allow a check to be made. Sheeting the loads was easy if the load was all full pallets of the same variety, but many loads were made up pallets of every variety and were up and down all over. Picking your way over loose trays of sauces and salad creams it was easy to put a foot in a hole and hurt yourself. We all had to work together in the late afternoon as there could be four or five loaded trailers waiting to be sheeted and roped or maybe with the sheets just draped over. All loads also had to have top sheet or skin on and in windy weather; it was easier to do this together.

Later that year John and I got a new unit apiece, mine came first, and John's about two weeks later. We had been told that they were MAN 240's and one was a day cab and the other a sleeper. John was a bit put out when we arrived at Johnstone one night and my new MAN was waiting for me, and I was to have the sleeper cab. It didn't really matter about the sleeper cab on nights but would be handy for a nap when on days, also the sleeper cab versions were better looking than the day cabs. John got his MAN later and for once, we were equals on the road. Although the cab on the MAN was very good, the engine performance was a let down. Again, the Atkinson Borderer and the 220 Cummins won hands down against the MAN 240. The column change had been replaced with a conventional gear stick and along with one or two minor things, it was the same as a 232. Like the Mercedes 1924, it suffered from a lack of guts and pulling power, granted it was better than the Mercedes in this respect and the cab was better but was still disappointing in performance. The fuel consumption was more or less the same as the Borderer unless it was windy and the load was high and then it was a bit thirsty. Still it was good to have a good comfortable cab with a radio that you could hear. The MAN did sound like a bag of spanners when ticking over, in fact they sounded very rough, not sounding at all like German engineering. The Volvo was given to Scotsman who had moved to Preston from Glasgow, the dreaded Mercedes was given to Frank, a distance driver at Preston depot.

Jack and Malcolms parted company that summer when Bob sacked him after trouble at Heinz. Bob had warned Jack about throwing spare sheets on the ground in the trailer park, but when Bob visited the factory, he again found some sheets under the wheels of a trailer. Jack had developed a careless attitude since his relegation to shunter at Heinz. I thought it was a bit harsh, but truth be known, Jack wanted to be away from Malcolms, for some reason he never settled and always wanted to return to Woodsides. I felt that I was losing a good mate; Jack was very good at cheering people up, a real comedian and a bit misunderstood by some drivers. As well as losing Jack, Ann and I went our separate ways, it was best really as she was getting very over-bearing and the talk of a future marriage certainly influenced my decision to part.

The same year I made yet another bad mistake, I left Malcolm's, a company and job I really liked. It was just a frame of mind thing, Jack leaving, Ann, divorce, one or two other issues got me in the wrong mindset, and as I have always done, I followed these feelings, right or wrong. I went to Smiths of Whiteinch, a small Glasgow company that ran two or three trunks between Lancashire and Glasgow. The trunkers were Lancashire drivers and I was to work on days shunting one of these trunks, changing over near the driver's house at Westhoughton. We had a good vehicle to do the job, a nearly new Volvo F88 290; this was to prove the only decent thing about the job. Most of the loads coming from Glasgow were steel coils or bright steel bars, the coils going to the Ford and Vauxhall car plants, the bars going to the Midlands. The coils were no problem, but the bars were terrible to deliver. If the right equipment had been used to load the bars on the trailer it would have been a lot easier. There was no attempt to separate the deliveries, and there could be four or five, so they were all lumped together. Invariably the bars had slipped and only the sheets were holding them on. Many times, I travelled to Birmingham with a massive bulge on one side of the trailer. At the drops, it was a dangerous job unsheeting and a few times some bars fell off. At the stockholders were I was unloading it meant asking the crane drivers to sort the load out for me, not always done agreeably. Five drops in the Midlands and then loading at ICI at Runcorn or Spillers at Birkenhead was a heavy day by Malcolm's standards.

When loading pet food at Spillers Birkenhead it was necessary to cover the load with a plastic sheet, as the Smith's sheets were suspect. The pallets were loaded two high and required at least three sheets to cover the load, with the plastic underneath. A top sheet was also put on and normally all this should have kept the load dry. It was a bit of a nightmare really, a plastic sheet with holes in it, worn out sheets on top and covered with a flimsy top sheet was all asking for trouble. But as usual, the driver got the blame and as usual, the driver had no say about the poor sheets.

Another regular back load was hydrated lime from Buxton, not a pleasant place to load at in bad weather. Late that year I arrived at the Buxton plant at around 3-30 in the afternoon, the weather was bad, wet, windy, snow in the air, and to cap it all there was a queue. When I finally got loaded, it was dark and it was now snowing quite heavily. All sheeting and roping had to be done outside, in the dark and in the carpet of white mud on the ground. Trying to sheet a low load with large sheets is easy in good weather, but trying to keep the sheets in the fold when it was windy was very nearly impossible. Of course, the wind got them and they trailed in the mud until I mastered them. After sheeting, I roped the load and spread the top sheet, sliding off the load holding a sheet tie; of course, the rest of the sheet blew off into the mess on the ground. After sorting that out, with sheet ties flicking muddy lime all over me, I was ready to go, or so I thought. After putting the lights on, I walked around the trailer to check everything and found that the trailer tail-lights were not working. Putting new bulbs in did not help, checking the plugs on the light lead, crawling in the mud under the trailer to see if any wires were out anywhere, checking fuses, all came to nothing. In an executive decision I put the hazard lights on and drove to Westhoughton were the trunker was waiting. We had another fiddle around trying to get the lights working but had no luck, so he set off to go to Glasgow with the hazards on. The next day he told me he had made it without being stopped by the police, very lucky I thought.

By now, Margaret had told me she was getting married again, to a schoolteacher, altogether a different bloke than me. She was moving to County Durham and our house was to be sold with a share going to me, I was to be in the money. I had myself moved on and was living in Blackburn with someone I had met in a club in Preston. Her name was Elizabeth and lived in a very nice bungalow with her young son and daughter. I felt quite settled with this arrangement; we had our nights out and occasionally bumped into Jack when in Preston. We had a good Christmas and as the New Year approached I was told that New Year's day was an ordinary day for English drivers and that we would be working, doing what I don't know. I disagreed with this as did the other drivers and said I would not work, thinking the others would back me up. It turned out that I was the only one not to work and for a week, nothing was said by the bosses. A week after New Year I had unloaded in Peterborough and was expecting a long day when I rang Glasgow for instructions. To my amazement they told me to get back to Westhoughton and that I was sacked. No reason was given, and I never asked, as I knew it was because I ducked on New Year's Day. I was not overly bothered especially as the sale of the house was imminent and there were other jobs. The job I got to tide me over was loading trailers in a paper mill near Blackburn, a job that did not last very long. One day I fell backwards off a trailer, I fell sitting down with my hands out behind me and although they both felt a bit painful, I carried on working until dinnertime. After dinner it was too painful to carry on so took myself to the hospital, after the X-rays I was told that I had broken the scaphoid bone in my right wrist and ripped the tendon on the thumb of the other. That was me off work for over two months, not something I liked at all. The money from the house sale came through and we all had a few days away just to make a change for us all.

I had been told that the plaster on one of my wrist could be on for up to ten weeks, I wanted to get back to work so after eight weeks I took the plaster off myself under the hot tap, they felt fine and have never given me any problems since.

It was time to bite the bullet and ask for my job back at Malcolms, not that I relished the idea of doing a bit of crawling. I was reasonably confident after my talk with Bob at Preston but he said he would have to consult Glasgow. The next day Bob rang and said it was alright and I could return, the only downside was that as I was to be last in, I had to go shunting in the Heinz factory on nights. It was only for a few months and being so relieved at getting my job back at Malcolms, it was something I accepted.

It was now 1980 and I had been working for nearly twenty years, practically all of it with extremely long hours and I was about to work in the Heinz factory on nights, not a thing to relish.

On nights at the Heinz factory meant loading, sheeting and roping four trailers and two rigid trucks. The rigids had to returned to Preston so it meant swapping them over during the night. I knew the system at the factory and soon got into a routine that worked best for me. Also in the factory at night was the B.R.S. shunter, an older man called Alf, and Tommy who shunted for Gaskells. Longs of Leeds had two drivers who made two trips a night from Leeds, loading a trailer each trip. A few other companies loaded one or two trailers early in the evening, so it was best to be at the factory by 7pm to be one of the first inside. Only four trailers were loaded before the break at 10pm, so it was important to be one of these four. The first rigid was loaded in a different area and was loaded and sheeted by 10pm and it was during the break I returned to Preston to get the other. If not many others turned up to be loaded, it was possible to have everything loaded, if not sheeted, by 3.30am or so. We were allowed to drop loaded trailers undercover, a practice not allowed on days and this helped a lot. The problems of wet and badly folded sheets made the job a lot harder. Malcolms had new top sheets that were very thick and had ropes instead of the usual thin sheet ties. When wet these sheets were hard to drag never mind lift but the fork truck drivers were very helpful, always allowing us to put them on top of a pallet before it was loaded. It did not take long for Tommy and me to become friends and decide to work as a team. W.J.

Ridings had a shunter on days and Tommy persuaded him to leave the keys for his old shunt wagon for us to use at night. With this unit we could have three trailers inside at 7 30pm and hopefully by the time Longs drivers arrived, three more. Tommy had six trailers to load but by working together, we had a good system. While I was away at Preston with the first rigid Tommy would weigh the loaded trailers and bring in, if possible, three more empties. If he had time, he would start sheeting a load until I returned to help. Alf the B.R.S. shunter agreed to join us and our little group all worked on any load.

Liz had sold her bungalow in Blackburn and we had bought a house together in Lytham St Annes. The house required some work on it and for a few months, it was all bed and work as I worked my way through the list of jobs to be done at home. Liz had a good Civil Service job and money was not a problem in those days even though all my money from Margaret was now tied up in this house.

The work in Heinz was telling on my legs and knees, walking on the concrete and jumping down off trailers made them quite sore sometimes. Alf had a nasty accident early one morning when he jumped off a pallet onto the trailer deck. As he landed, a rotten plank on the trailer floor gave way and his leg went through. The jagged edges rolled the skin off the inside of his leg practically up to his groin, he was in a bad way and an ambulance had to be called for him. Alf was off work for a few weeks and his replacement was not interested in working together so Tommy and I left him to it. Not long after Alf returned to work, it was my turn for another accident. It was around 2.30 am and we were dashing around, Tommy was moving trailers and I was sheeting loads at the top of the warehouse. I was working on a Malcolm's trailer and after spreading the front sheet; I jumped down and threw the front corner sheet ties across the front of the trailer. When I pulled the tie, it came out of its hole and I staggered backwards, ending up sitting down against the front wheel nuts of another shunt wagon. Tommy had heard me shout and dashed over to help me stand, as soon as I stood up I knew it was pretty bad. I had to undo my belt, as the pain in my back was awful; it felt like my back was swelling up already. Tommy walked me down to see the Heinz nurse who said I should go to hospital, I refused this but as any more work was impossible, Tommy helped me into the Malcolm's rigid and I painfully drove back to Preston. I nearly fell out of the cab, rolled into my car, and made for home. On arriving, I could hardly stand up but somehow got into the house. After hearing my shout Liz came down to help me, she also said I should go the hospital and I again refused, saying I would see what it was like in the morning. The next day it was no contest, it was the hospital for me, half-walking, half very nearly crawling. After X-Rays it was found that I had chipped the bone at the bottom of my spine, so that was that, off work again. Over the next few weeks the bruising spread all over my back, it looked a real mess and coupled with the swelling I was very nearly immobile. I could not sit properly, lie on my back and everything was a major effort. It took around six weeks before I could return to work, not really long enough, but I thought I was okay.

Not a great deal of sympathy was offered from the office, so it was back to the Heinz factory until my saviour, a new driver came along. My back has never been the same since and definitely does not like the cold. The work in Heinz was only four nights and on the fifth I did a Glasgow trunk, which made the week a bit easier. Tommy, Alf and I were soon back in our old routine, and few weeks later a miracle happened, a new driver started at Malcolms, I was out of Heinz after just six months.

I was going on distance and for this I got a MAN 240, it was not very old and was very tidy inside and out, I was quite chuffed with it. That weekend I gathered everything I would need; a little cooker; gas bottle; sleeping bag and bedding; toiletries; and a host of other items including a 12-volt TV. Distance drivers at Preston rarely travelled north as the Scottish drivers and the night trunks covered this work. We covered all of England and Wales, with London being the most visited. Malcolm's had an office behind the café at South Mimms, where there was plenty of space to park at night.

At around 5-30am on the Monday morning I arrived at the depot with all my kit, including a couple of Tesco bags filled with essentials and goodies. I was going to London, south of the Thames with a load of spirits on pallets, and after sorting my cab out, hooking up and checking the trailer, I was ready by six o'clock. I was travelling with two other Preston drivers, Eric and Frank who were both good mates of mine, Eric had a MAN and Franks the Mercedes that I had used on nights. We got through the heavy traffic around Birmingham and stopped at Corley services for our break, Eric and Frank were going into Kent but we would all probably be at South Mimms that night though. This was not the case for me as when I had tipped I went to Purfleet to load plywood for Lancashire. That night I stayed on a large lay-by on the A13, not ideal, but I had no time left. The M25 was only open in a few sections and not fully open until the mid-1980s, so driving through parts of London was unavoidable, a thing that never really bothered me as I found it interesting. Arriving back in Lancashire the next day I tipped my trailer and spent the rest of the day at the Heinz factory. Tommy the

Gaskells shunter had seen the light and was Malcolm's day shunter in the factory, like everyone before him, he wanted to be on the road and out of Heinz. I told Tommy to bide his time and it would happen within a few months, it always had in the past.

The months went by with no problems, the work was good and it was possible to spend time with your mates, either on the same job or parked together in an evening. Malcolm's had some of their own work in the London area but some work came from other sources, paper reels for newsprint being one of them. To load newsprint at Purfleet we had to have a number of chocks, a back scotch, and a nail free well planked trailer deck. Before going to Purfleet the scotches had to be collected from an office in Whitechapel, I think the office had set up a deposit system for the hire of the chocks. The problem was that sometimes we not tip the loads so the scotches disappeared into the ether, never to be seen again. We did try to carry them with us but that only worked out now and again.

There was an occasion, on a Friday, when the South Mimms depot was struggling to find enough back loads for everyone. We had hung around, waiting for the manager to find a load here and there, until, in the early afternoon it was just too late for anything to turn up. I think the manager had admitted defeat when four Preston drivers were told to go a local transport yard, and use their ramp to piggyback two units and trailers, as by now nothing was going to turn up. I had a newish Montracon trailer and Eric drove up the ramp and onto my trailer. There was about a six-foot overhang but with marker boards and lights it was still legal. Smurf drove onto Frank's trailer and promptly went through a bad board; we sorted this out and then chained the trailers to each other.

By this time it was well after four in the afternoon, it was a Friday and the M1 had massive road works going on, not a good combination. By 7 o'clock, we had only reached Corley services and we all agreed to stay on the services that night, at least we would get a Saturday morning out of it. I remember telling Eric not to forget where he was if he got up in the night, it was a long way to fall if he did forget.

The area behind the café at South Mimms where our Portacabin was got very muddy in winter, this got the cab floor messy so when the garage shut some of us would move to the top and park on the garage fore-court. Opposite the garage was a very long lay-by and this was usually full of lorries parked for the night, you had to be early to get on this lay-by. A funny episode occurred early one morning when Smurf accidentally locked himself out of his cab.

He had got up for a leak, and was standing outside when the cab door slammed shut, he must not have had the door catch set right as it locked itself, leaving Smurf stood in the cold dressed in his underclothes. We had to break in to the cab to get him back to his bed, it was very comical to see 5foot 3 inch tall Smurf stood there in his underpants and boots on his feet, comical for us, but not for Smurf.

In early 1982, the Falklands war was about to start and quantities of steel plates were being delivered to the Royal Naval Dockyard at Plymouth. I delivered a load of plates, but never got the chance to see much of the dockyard, and was a bit disappointed, but I got another chance a few weeks later. Frank and I delivered two cherry pickers to the dockyard; I think to be used for working on the ships hulls. After unloading we were chatting to a naval officer about the dockyard and the warships when, unexpectedly, he asked us we would like a bit of a tour. The officer drove us round in a navy Landrover, we saw many of the warships, and we even got near to the submarines. It was a fascinating look at the Navy, which by now was on a war footing.

Malcolms were now delivering not just to London but into Kent as well, all from the Heinz factory at Wigan. Before all Malcolm's work from Heinz was usually for Scotland and later to London, so this extra work was a boost for Preston depot. As well as delivering the Heinz loads to supermarket warehouses, there were many loads destined for another Heinz factory at Harlesden just off the North Circular, these loads were known as branch loads. They were usually full loads of one variety; salad cream, sauces, soups or baked beans. Many loads of Heinz also went the Tesco main warehouse at Hoddesdon, a place that at the time was a reasonably quick tip.

Where drivers parked up at night was, since the arrival of sleeper cabs and the demise of many of the transport digs, a matter of personnel choice. Everyone had their preferences, some preferred the motorway services, others lay-by's or quiet spots on industrial areas. Parking on the motorway services was at the time a bit of a jumbled up mess, drivers parked anywhere and the next morning you could find yourself surrounded, unable to get out easily, now it is more regimented and a lot tidier. If I was on my own I preferred a lay-by that ran away from the road, it was quieter and not buffeted by passing traffic. Lorry parks were alright, it was a bit noisy sometimes, especially the parks being used for changeovers at night. Northampton lorry park was a place I used a lot, but even here, it was impossible to avoid the inconsiderate drivers. I was parked at Northampton one winter's night, and was awoken in the early hours by my neighbour. He started his engine and had it running on high revs, this went on for ten minutes or so, until I reached out through my cab window and banged on his cab door. His excuse was that he was cold and I shouted back that most of us were probably cold but were not all starting our engines. Not many drivers had night heaters; some still did not have sleeper cab units, not counting the Atkinson's with the coffin behind the cab. The MAN cab was cold and not very well insulated, I felt the cold coming through the back of the cab and it was not good for my bad back. At South Mimms, after a very cold frosty night, the inside of the windscreen was frozen and at one point, we thought we might have to get an ambulance for a driver. We could not seem to be able to wake him up properly, we started his engine, made tea for him, but it took a while for him to recover. My television picked up CB radio traffic on some lorry parks, a bit annoying listening to the rubbish being passed around. I did have a CB in the late 70s before they were legalized, but never got the hang of it and dumped it. Not many Malcolm's drivers seemed to be CB addicts; before 1981 a few had them confiscated on motorway services as they were caught using the illegal sets. Sleeper cabs gave drivers, if properly equipped, a home from home and the days of the transport digs, good and bad were nearly over, along with good nights out that we all had.

We were getting some good work now, work that was our own and not through another company, work out of London tended to be a poor rate as it was passed on down the line so to speak. Malcolms had started loading structural steelwork from Condor at Eastleigh, a place I visited a few times. One summer's day when enroute to Eastleigh I was coming down the down the Winchester bypass, I had my window open as it was very warm, when suddenly I heard a sort of plop noise by my right ear. Looking round I was shocked to see a huge green and yellow insect clinging to the curtain by my head. The bypass was not a wide carriageway and I must have wandered a bit whilst trying to shake this monster insect off the curtain, it eventually disappeared, but I knew not where, was it outside, or was it still in the cab. On reaching the Condor factory I was too late to load that day and spent half an hour emptying the cab just to check the monster had gone, no way did I want to wake up in the night with that crawling on me. Ray Skupski who I was at Northern Ireland Trailers with, was about to leave the factory heading for Fleetwood, he had transferred to from N.I.T. to Pandora a few years before. We had a good chat and a laugh about the insect; it was good to see old friends again. The next morning I loaded a complete roof and supports for a garage forecourt in Scarborough, to be on site by 9 am the following day. I was on time in Scarborough the next day and never saw the monster insect again.

Around this time, Frank had an accident that potentially could have been serious. Malcolms loaded Hi-Mac excavators at Rhymney in South Wales, the excavators loaded were either the wheeled or the tracked type. The tracked excavators were driven up a ramp onto a normal flat trailer, the tracks being placed over the trailer axles and the excavator arm extended out to the headboard. After being chained over the tracks and under the trailer chassis, they were good to go, a bit high on the middle of the arm, but ok for most A road bridges. Unfortunately, Frank's load hit a bridge near Queensferry, the load was wedged under the bridge and the road was closed off. No serious damage was done to the bridge or excavator and it would have been forgotten except for a Ministry poster.

The poster was stuck on the wall by the time clock and depicted a lorry stuck under a railway bridge, with passenger carriages strewn down the embankment, a worst case scenario if ever there was one. Some wit had written on the poster "Frank-Demolition Contractor", Frank had to look at this poster for months after.

Malcolms left the depot at South Mimms and moved to a new location opposite the old Bell Bar Café near Hatfield. The depot had a small compound along with a building large enough to get two or three trailers inside. The café opposite had now closed down so there was plenty of parking almost opposite the new depot. Trunks would be running from Hatfield to Preston and return, with three trunks from Preston doing the opposite journey. By now Preston had Scania 111 units for the trunks, London depot receiving the same units for their trunks. At Preston, a strange Scania unit arrived that proved to be a test vehicle for Scania. The cab was very small, a day cab with no markings on the front grills except for the Scania name and was in the Malcolm's livery. The small unit was very deceiving; its power was unlike any other unit at Preston. Coming over the M62 from Yorkshire to Lancashire it could, even when fully loaded, pass any of us with ease. We never found out what the engine in the odd unit was, and it departed after a few months, presumably back to Scania.

Near the point where the A11 meets the A13 in Whitechapel, a large office block with car parking was being constructed. Fifty foot concrete beams came down to Preston from Glasgow at night and Preston drivers took the loads onto London. Because of the traffic problems around the construction site the council banned any unloading till after six in the evening. There was a danger of the beams swinging out into the road when being lifted;

one driver through no fault of his own had the awful sight of watching a beam miss a London bus by a few inches. I did this job quite a few times, mainly after running back into Preston depot just before dinner. It was best to arrive on site around 5-30 to 6 pm as we were parked on the road to unload. At that time of the day all the workers had finished, except for the tower crane driver and a foreman. The foreman nearly always gave the drivers a tenner if we would shackle the beams onto the wires, and using a walkie- talkie, give instructions to the crane driver. When the building became seven or eight stories high the crane driver could not see us, nor could we see him. One particular evening the crane driver came down to see me and tell me what he required, he was a very young Irish man with gold earrings, spotless jeans and a pure white tee shirt; I thought he looked a bit like David Essex. The first beam we lifted swung a bit, but the unloading went without a hitch, mainly due to the crane driver's skill at his job, the speed he took the beams up was unbelievable. When he came down to see me he was smiling and looking like he was off out for the evening, a very skilled young man.

PHOTO COURTESY OF BILL REID

Tommy was now out of the Heinz factory and on distance work, I was very pleased for him, he was good company, was always cheerful and ready to help anyone. Tommy was a bit different in some ways, he never had food at night and I shared my dinner with him sometimes. He also seemed to attract grease and mud; sometimes it looked as if he had been cleaning the fifth wheel. He liked a drink and it took ages to get him up in a morning, but moments after seeing his face behind the curtain he was ready to go. Maybe his way was better than mine, all the tidying and dusting I did before I would move was a bit much.

Elizabeth and I had finally got married in a quiet registry office wedding in Blackpool. We had a few days away on the South Coast, which was very relaxing except for the drive there. Liz could drive and was probably a very good driver, it was just that I did not being driven by anyone, and I felt more at ease driving myself. Liz insisted on driving and it was impossible to change her mind, so I had to sit and be quiet. We had a good time though, and she did let me drive home.

Three drivers from Preston including myself had a pleasant three days in Southampton that summer, and all in glorious weather. We had left Preston all loaded with 45-foot steel pipes for the docks in Southampton. On the journey down, we saw many other Scottish lorries hauling the same pipes so we knew there would be a queue at the docks. Arriving at the docks we found ourselves behind at least 25 other lorries all loaded with the steel pipes. As the day went on the queue hardly moved, we walked down to the head of the line of lorries to see what, if anything was happening. The tubes had to be loaded onto wheeled Ro-Ro flats that would be put in the hold of a ferry. Steel goal post were needed on the flats to keep the pipes secure, the problem being, they did not have any. We were told a local company was urgently making the goal post but it was going to take some time for any quantity to appear. There was nothing anyone could do about it, but the weather was great so we made the best of it. Only a handful of loads were tipped that day and there was a bit of grumbling by some drivers. After the dockers finished for the day we asked if there were any showers in the dock area, a docker told us that some slipper baths were not far away. Eric, Frank and I walked down to the baths and it was great to have a good soak. The baths were huge, the water hot, and it was quiet cheap really. That night we had a meal and a couple of drinks and it felt like we were on our holidays. Next day the queue moved slowly and it was looking doubtful that we would be unloaded on this, the second day. Eric and I had a walk round to the cruise liner terminal, one of the biggest liners I had ever seen was on the berth, another dock nearby held two large liners that looked very neglected, I think one of them was the Canberra, it was all very interesting to both of us. The unloading was going a bit better but it was obvious that it was going to be the next day before any of our trio would be empty. It was after dinner on the third day before Eric was the first to be unloaded, it did not take long to unload, it was the lack of equipment that caused the delay. With all three of us empty, Eric was told to load at Purfleet while Frank and I went up to the depot at Hatfield. It had made a nice change waiting at the docks but with no overtime or bonus, it did hit our wages somewhat.

Everyone got on well with each other at Preston depot, either working in the yard, at the Heinz factory or on the road, but there was always someone you took a dislike to, no matter where you worked. We never really had drivers meetings until this particular driver started, he could not wait to mention that he had been a shop steward and what a big union man he was. For no reason at all it was decided to have a drivers meeting one Saturday morning, as far as I knew we had nothing to complain about and it seemed a bit pointless to me. Straight away, the ex-shop steward wanted to be in charge, aggressively arguing against some working practices or conditions. We were nearly all T.G.W.U. apart from a couple who were with the United Road Transport Union. He wanted everyone to be in the T.G.W.U. as he said some docks did not accept the U.R.T.U; he did have a point as certainly Hull Docks favoured this. It was just his attitude that got up my nose, to me it smacked of big brother. After a few other minor issues were turned into major ones, I called him a "Red stirrer", neither of us wanted to go on any job together after that. It was only my opinion but there was not much to complain about at Malcolms, certainly nothing to upset anyone.

It was around middle of the eighties that I began developing very severe headaches, I was sent for a head scan, which brought back the spectre of my old head injury from a few years before. I had banged my head again a few months previously so it was a bit worrying. I had walked into a girder that was sticking out of the back of a trailer, not even a Malcolm's trailer at that. I had seen stars when I hit my head and cut my forehead but apart from being a bit dizzy I soon got over it. The scan showed a slight bleed on a blood vessel in my head but they could not determine how old the bleed was. I received more tablets and the headaches went away after a couple of weeks or so. I was not too bothered once the head aches had gone and it was no use worrying.

More Tautliners were in use by now, they were excellent for certain jobs but were not good in windy weather. I followed Concorde over the Thelwall Viaduct one very windy day, his trailer was empty and as one strong gust hit the trailer, I thought it was going over. Concorde said afterwards he going over the viaduct in the middle lane next time. Low bridges were a problem; I think we had some Tautliners that were over fifteen foot high. It is the norm nowadays but they were new to us at the time.

The majority of our work was still on flat trailers with the sheets and ropes. The standards of this lost art was very good at Malcolms, we all gave each other marks out of ten for good sheeting and roping. I remember coming into the yard one afternoon with a bit of loose sheet on one corner of my load, Frank was very quick to award me a five, saying it was not up to my usual standard. Some drivers never got the hang of sheeting a trailer and some loads were a real mess. It was easy enough with a nice level twenty pallet load; the secret was to sheet loads that were up and down and awkward shapes. Industrial machinery was a very difficult load to sheet, impossible to walk on, gaps between the machines and sharp parts to cut the sheets. The Chrysler car part stillages or any stillages were particularly difficult and dangerous to sheet. I never forgot the Caledonian driver sheeting up at the Weyroc factory in Annan twenty odd years before.

Basically, general haulage means just that, at Malcolms we carried anything at all, mostly on flat trailers. I once loaded a large Volvo articulated dumper that even then I thought was a bit much for a flat trailer, nowadays it would have gone on a low-loader. I remember having to keep stopping to tighten the chains as the dumper had a mind of its own. Occasionally we did a bit of container work from Tilbury but it was very rare, Scottish drivers did more of this work north of the border. Sometimes errors are made, some more costly than others and I was no exception. I was sent to load two Portacabins at the factory just outside York, it was late in the afternoon when I arrived and the loaders were non-too pleased. The cabins had to be loaded that night as I was to change over with a Glasgow driver early the next morning, a bit further up the A1. The two cabins were going on a fifty foot trailer so there was plenty of room, but for once, this trailer had no timbers on it, I was scratching around the loading yard for any old bits of wood. The first cabin to be loaded sat on my bits of timber and the cabin edges cleared the chock rail ok, the second one only had some inferior timber under it but still cleared the chock rail. Without even asking, the loaders had unhooked the cabin and had dashed away. It was one of those things; it looked okay, but could be better. I changed over with the Glasgow driver the next morning, the cabins had to be delivered that day so he had plenty of time to spare. When I got back to Preston that night Bob called me into the office and told me the worst. One of the cabins had sunk down on the bad timbers, the electric cables running underneath the cabin had rubbed and chaffed on the chock rail, ruining the whole wiring. There is not much you can say really, it would all sound like made up excuses, but no one likes making mistakes.

I had a short spell on London trunk for no other reason than a change for a while. There was some swapping and changing all the time at Malcolm's and Bob the manager always agreed to any request made by the drivers. That is not to say Bob was an easy touch but that his management skills were very good. He was a big man with a soft Scottish voice, but no one ever crossed him and he had our respect.

Three trunks went to Hatfield five nights a week and although the mileage was a bit less than a Glasgow trunk it proved to be a more difficult journey. Dave Morley who was one of the other London night drivers was a good friend of mine, we could always have a laugh about most things when we had been on days together. The traffic was heavier going south, it made the Glasgow trunk seem very quiet in comparison. When we arrived at the Hatfield depot we had to struggle in the dark with the king-pin locks that had to be on the trailers at all times. Sometimes the locks came off easily, other times they would not budge at all. We kept a spare pair of gloves for this job, they were no use for anything else once coated with grease, and we could even get grease on our hair if we were not careful. The yard at the depot was very small and only allowed us to park up one at a time, it was not easy in the pitch dark. We all had Scania 111's which were a vast improvement on the MAN 240's, also as we were all equally matched it made a nice change for me. In the time on Glasgow trunk I never encountered any road closures, but in six months on the London trunk the M1 was closed about three times. One M1 closure took us off the motorway and through Milton Keynes to Northhampton, it was surprising how much traffic built up in the very early hours. Traffic accidents were more common going south, even taking into account the lighter traffic there were very few accidents going north. The weather could be worse going north, I had done the Glasgow trunk with thick fog for much of the journey, we even followed the snow plough up Beatock one night but we always got there and back without any of the other hassles going south threw up. The wind never seemed as bad going south but taking everything into account I would much rather go north than south. I suppose this is why I only did the south trunk for around six months.

It was better to be back on distance work, the London trunk was okay but six months of it was proving a bit boring. A few Scania 112's were arriving at Preston, one low cab and two high cab versions, these Scania's were on trunk so apart from my old Mercedes 1924 which Frank drove, all the distance drivers were on the MAN 240's. I got another MAN which had come off nights so it was not very old and had been looked after. One of the draw-backs of being on nights was missing familiar faces, I saw some of them if they were in the depot in an evening but a few I hardly ever saw. The Scottish drivers were great to get on with, they always seemed to be content with everything and always very humorous. One of my favourites was Jim Mclaren, he was an old hand at Malcolms and was always one of the first drivers to get the latest unit. Sometimes it was difficult to know if he was serious or just joking, it was usually the latter. Jim was ten or twelve years older than me and had probably forgotten more than I knew at the time, he was certainly one of a special breed that is no more nowadays. The image of a hard, rough Glaswegian lorry driver does not stand up, practically all the drivers I met were very witty, good company and very helpful. W H Malcolm built his extremely successful and large company with Scottish lorry drivers, many years before any drivers south of the border worked for him, some drivers spent there working life at the company. The whole experience of working for the company was something I am glad I did.

Preston depot was always busy and we were lucky to have the Heinz factory so close to Preston. A lot more timed deliveries were taking place including the Heinz, spirits and bottles. Most of the timed deliveries were easy to handle as we always had enough time to arrive early enough for our slot. The bottles to Schweppes at Sidcup were sometimes one load every hour, this was mostly in summer when production was very high. Bottles from Rockware and U.G.B. played a huge part in our work, many loads coming from Johnstone which had large storage and warehouse facilities. Knottingley and Doncaster bottles were loaded mostly for Scotland and left Preston on the trunks.

Everyone that a person works with is usually classed as a workmate, but there is always a smaller circle that are closer friends. Tommy was one of these stemming from our nights in the Heinz factory, John, Alan, Frank, Martin and Dave were also good friends. Eric, who was quite a bit older than me was one of my favourites, if Eric and I were going away together it was always a good two or three days out. Eric was a very calm person, never got worked up or angry and was always spot on in everything he did, I tend to be a bit hot tempered and soon got agitated, something I have been told that started with my head injury.

More new Scanias 112s were arriving at Preston, all of these went on the Glasgow and London trunks. A Scania 112 also came to Preston and it sat in the yard for a couple of days until I was told that it was mine. I was the first day driver to get a 112, I don't know why I was chosen, there were drivers senior to me, I expected the calls of "Blue Eyes" that I had got at N.I.T. when I got the Borderer, but I never heard a grouse from anyone. The 112 had been used by a Johnstone driver who had moved onto a new Volvo F12, it had been looked after and was totally unmarked. By now the 38 ton weight limit had been in force for a while and 38 tons was a bit of a struggle for the MAN 240 which was the main distance unit at Preston.

The Scottish drivers were way ahead of Preston depot, having the F10/12, MAN 280, DAF 3300 and the Scania 112 so all in all I was well pleased to have the Scania. The first time I took the 112 out I joined the motorway at Leyland and was overtaken by Eric in his car. He was going on holiday with his family and as he passed me, waving and laughing, I got my cloth and pretended to be dusting the cab. Eric shot away from me waving his arm out of the window, good old Eric. Not long after I got the Scania it was sent to Carlisle to have a tag axle fitted, when it came back I was a bit disappointed with the conversion. When the axle was raised it was only a couple of inches off the ground, the fitter at Preston said it should be more than that but that's how it stayed. The axle was very narrow with single wheels and I thought the whole thing spoilt the look of the Scania.

Most of our work was for the south and all return loads were through the Hatfield depot, some good, and some bad. A decent return load that got us back to Birmingham was drums of oil from Texaco at the Isle of Grain refinery near Rochester. The oil was for a Texaco depot at the side of the M 5 at West Bromwich, a good place to tip, arrive at 8am and empty by 9am everytime.

At the Hatfield depot we had plenty of parking on the old café opposite and there was usually two or three of us there most nights. I still used Northampton for parking up but stopped using the lorry park. I found a road on a trading estate near to the brewery, it got a bit full some nights and sometimes meant reversing down the cul-de-sac to find a spot, but it was a lot better than the lorry park. I also used Toddington services quite often despite the noise and the knocks on the door late at night from the certain ladies who frequented some services at the time. Further north Walsall was a decent little lorry park but being small it was sometimes full, then it was the last resort for me, Keele services.

One of the things that annoyed a bit at Hatfield depot was the habit of them taking your load off you and sending it on trunk The manager would drag us from places in the south that were way off the depot, I remember loading steelwork at Condor near Eastleigh and after ringing to say I was loaded got usual message "I need that load for trunk". This happened many, many times and sometimes it felt totally idiotic and must have reduced the profit on the load. Work was hard to find in the south, maybe someone from London should have been out looking for the right work.

A terrible accident happened one morning at the old Bell Bar Café lorry park we used opposite the Hatfield depot. Tommy and I had loaded at Heinz in Harlesden and had been brought back to the depot. I am not sure what happened to our loads but we were not travelling together the next day. I had fuelled up in the depot before Tommy, and had parked up over the road. I had walked down to the phone kiosk near the pub which was very near the café, and saw Tommy leave the depot to park up. I finished my call and walked back to the café where Tommy was nowhere to be seen, he was not in his cab so I presumed he had gone to the pub and I had missed him. This was not unusual for Tommy and we sometimes went for a drink together. I did not fancy a drink that night so I went for a wash at the depot and then made something to eat. I watched the television until bedtime and never saw Tommy return to the café. The next morning I got up and prepared to leave, Tommy's lorry was not close to mine and for reasons I cannot explain I never went to get Tommy up. In the dark I could just make out a figure sat in the passenger seat, the dim cab light was on and it

125

appeared to me that Tommy was awake and getting ready to move. Not travelling together was maybe why I didn't go across to him, but I will never know really. I was delivering in London that day and when I rang the depot I was given the shocking news, Tommy was dead. It was not until later in the day when I arrived back at the depot that I found out the extent of the tragedy. It was deduced by the police that Tommy had stayed at the pub a good while the previous evening. On his return to the café he had lit his gas stove, it was a cold night and we all knew the dangers, but many of us have done this at sometime. Tommy must have fallen asleep with the stove lit and in his sleep had been overcome by the stoves fumes. The horrible news was compounded when I saw Tommy's gear in a pile on the shed floor. When I asked about this I was told to take it back to Preston with me, I then saw a Scania seat in the shed and asked where Tommy's unit was, I was told they had washed it out and it was working in London. I was very upset and angry at this explanation, it would not have happened at Preston and definitely not in Scotland. Tommy's unit was supposed to be returned to Preston but as far as I remember we never had it back, we didn't really want it. One minute people are there and the next they are gone forever, and all because of an error of judgement. Tommy was a unique bloke with a unique life style, a cracking worker and a good friend to many, many other drivers. As the saying goes "Life goes on" and so it did without poor Tommy.

The months turned into a couple of years with the same routine, long hours, grabbing the overtime, taking a few chances and generally loving it and hating some of the time. I was now in my forties and was starting to think "What's it all about" and looking for something different. A couple of things happened that swayed me to these thoughts, both of which were close together. Bob our manager at Preston went home one night and had a stroke, he recovered but never returned to work, another good bloke to not see again. The second thing tied in with our move to a new larger depot at the top of Bamber Bridge, it was a lot better place with room to move and a larger shed for transhipping at night. The second main happening was the arrival of our new manager, a man that some, including myself took an instant dislike to. Bob, our now retired manager was a down to earth man, he came to work in his old car dressed in his baggy cords and cardigan. Our new manager swept into the yard in his flash car with the two aerials on the back and all dressed up in his flash suit. He was a young Englishman from another Glasgow company, I think we would have preferred to have another Scot as manager just to keep the continuity going. Things were changing and he was the man to do it, he seemed to change things for the sake of it, some of us saw all this as not to our liking, for myself I thought that I would wait and see how it panned out.

Occasionally we did get a trip north of the border but they were very rare, I went to Johnstone once with a load and just changed trailers. I was given a steel load with five drops in the midlands. We got these multi-drops now and again, personally I didn't mind them, it kept you out of the way for a while. But it was still London that most of us went to every week and to go somewhere different made a nice change. I loaded another full filling station canopy at Condor near Eastleigh and fully expected to be told to return to Hatfield with the load. This time the canopy was for a garage in Lancaster, okay it was near Preston but it was better to be told to travel with the load. We got a fair bit of work out of the Condor works, a few times especially if we happened to have a fifty foot trailer, and were in the area, we were sent to Condor. It took a few hours loading but I believe the rate was very good. Most of us carried a couple of marker boards and lights as you didn't want to miss a load because of lack of equipment. One load I got from Condor was fifty five foot long and about ten foot wide, I had four chains and dwangs and plenty of markers, it took a good while to prepare the load but it was well secured and lit up like Christmas tree.

Frank and I travelled to Ipswich one day with loaded containers, we did a little bit of container work, mainly from Tilbury so Ipswich was a nice change, made even better with the knowledge that we were to back load containers from Ipswich. Frank and I had a good couple of days and we got two nights out from the job. We got quite a lot of whisky and gin through Preston for delivery anywhere in the south. The only times I visited Felixstowe was with whisky, mostly on pallets but once loaded on the deck, it was a bit of hard work but easy to load the pallets once a rhythm was established.

Hatfield depot was finding back loads from somewhere, we were doing baled waste paper and card, scaffolding, inner door car panels for Vauxhall, timber, paper, steel coils from London steel terminal and empty containers from Tilbury for Coatbridge which probably just paid for the fuel. In fact we loaded anything which is what general haulage was all about. I loaded mahogany tree trunks from around the Epsom area, I had a pair of goalpost and when the loader put forty five foot mahogany tree trunk on the trailer a little too severely I thought the trailer was going to tip over. It didn't take many of the tree trunks to make a heavy load, I was hoping to travel with the load myself, but no, I was back at Hatfield that night, it was wanted for the trunks and my overtime was reduced yet again.

At Preston depot there were rumours of one or two drivers going in the office as traffic clerks, the names mentioned did not surprise me and did not fill me with delight. It was bad enough going in the office and seeing our new manager without looking at faces that I had never got on with. Harry, who had worked with Bob in the office for many years was the only friendly face and I think even he must have not relished the huge changes. I suppose in a way it was a sign of the times, everything was getting more controlled and regimented, we were losing the easy going way of working, a way that still got the job done. When I look at companies like Stobarts and to a lesser extent Malcolms in 2014, I honestly think that I could not work as a lorry driver in 2014. The present day lorries (Trucks) are so far removed from my ERF with the 150 Gardner engine, I would like to drive a present day truck, but only if I could take it back forty odd years, now that would be something. Some people find it hard to move with the times and I am afraid I am one of them. I felt that somehow I wanted to go back to an earlier time, when things were simpler and dare I say it easier, today the 21st century does not do a lot for me.

The final thing that made my mind up to go for a change came about one day in London. I was sent to load newsprint at Purfleet, the weather that day was awful, with wind and torrential rain that looked in for the day. After hanging around at Purfleet I was loaded outside in a brief respite from the rain. The reels did not make a full load, probably around twelve tons, so thinking our office knew this I sheeted and roped the load putting a plastic sheet on first, by this time it was raining again. After getting my notes I rang Hatfield, the manager was surprised that I only had a part load. He then shocked me by telling me to off-load the reels as he said he had nothing to make the load up with. The office at Purfleet were none too pleased at my request to off-load but agreed to do it in a while. When they were ready I took the sheets off in a lake of water as the rain had abated a little, the sheets were wet before but now they were saturated. I folded the sheets and could hardly drag them never mind lift them but got a fork truck to lift them on the trailer for me. Ringing Hatfield again I was told to ring again in an hour which would make it around 1-30pm by then. After dinner I rang again and was told to give it another hour and ring again. At 2-45 pm they told me I was to get to Sheerness as fast as possible, my immediate thought was great, I was going to load steel re-enforcing rods in Sheerness, this was not to be as he said I was loading oranges at Sheerness for Glasgow. I told him the sheets were sopping wet but their response was that it would be okay with the plastic on first. The thought "You're the boss" came in my head so I did not argue and set off for Sheerness. It was a Friday and the traffic was bad so it was after 4-30 pm when I arrived in Sheerness. I was loaded in one of the sheds by just after 5 pm or so, quite fast really, but was then told I would have to sheet and rope outside as they were closing the shed. It was throwing it down outside but there was nothing for it but to pull out of the shed with no sheets on the load. Outside it was pitch dark, windy and raining heavily so it was a struggle to keep the plastic sheet in place until the other sheets were spread. The pallets of oranges were quite high which didn't help, but I managed it somehow, the ropes showered me with dirty water making me even wetter than before. I spread the top-sheet and slid down the load holding a tie to try to keep it on the load, the wind came up and blew the top-sheet off before I had a chance to secure a couple of ties. I wrapped it up and had to ask another driver for a lift to get it back on the load. The driver I asked was a gem, he stayed with me in the rain until we had the skin secured, it may not have been possible without his help, he was yet another dying breed of driver.

I had to get fuel at a R.T.A. company close by and this done I made it to Toddington services by 8-00pm just about dried out. The load had to be in Preston as early as possible on Saturday morning for a Scottish driver to take it north. I arrived at Preston depot by 9-30am the next day to find the Scottish driver waiting for me. I left for home at around mid-day thinking all was well and looking forward to the weekend. On the Monday I was only going local and was back in the yard with a Heinz load by mid-afternoon. I was immediately summoned to the office to see the manager, who told me the load of oranges had been rejected and asked for an explanation for this. Telling him about the circus on Friday, the saturated sheets, the comments I made to Hatfield about the sheets and my position outside at Sheerness did no good. I was told the onus was on me to keep the load dry which I very nearly replied with "don't talk stupid rubbish", I kept my mouth shut but was very angry that I was being blamed. For me it was the final straw, Liz and I had a plan and this episode brought it to the front of my thinking.

CHAPTER FIVE
FULL CIRCLE

My sister and her family were living in West Wales, deep in the countryside and having a great time living a bit simpler life. Our house in St. Annes was almost sold and we planned to go to Wales and at first just to rent a place in the country.

The day came and I gave my notice in at Malcolms, maybe not a thing I would have done with Bob still as manager but I could not work with the new man and as I said I totally disliked him. It was all great for 98% of the time at Malcolms, no complaints at all and I would do it again if I could go back a good few years. It was sad to be leaving everyone (Well nearly everyone) but I was looking forward to a new challenge and new horizons.

We had found a small cottage to rent in a tiny village called Llanpumsaint just to the north of Carmarthen. It had a very large garden and a small stream at the side but best of all we had no neighbours. We were only renting it as I really wanted to live in Pembrokeshire but it be great for the time being. Liz had a job to go to and as I still had to work I started asking around the village for any openings. If anyone wants to work it was there for the finding, within a week I was working on a casual basis for the builder in the village and also doing a few school runs with a mini-bus for a small outfit near the village. Someone told me about a haulage contractor in the next village of Alltwalis called Charles Footman, so I paid him a visit and got another casual job. At first working for Footmans was just delivering fertilizer to farms in S.W. Wales, for these deliveries I drove a Leyland 2 axle rigid and a Volvo F86 3 axle rigid. It was hard work and the farms were even harder to find but I enjoyed it really as there was no pressure and not much traffic to cope with. The early Pembrokeshire potato season was about to start and Mr. Footman told me I would be needed a lot more once this started.

When the potato season started Footman's artics went to farms and loaded the potatoes straight out of the fields. I took an artic down to a farm near Neyland in Pembrokeshire, I had a mate to help with the loading as it was all handball work. I had loaded spuds before and once the loading started it was surprising how quickly twenty four tons of potatoes could be loaded in a nice neat fashion. After loading we went back to the depot and another driver took it onwards. This work went on for weeks and odd times I took a load to the London market, once loading spuds back to Wales from near Cambridge, I thought that rather strange, surely they had enough spuds in Wales. When the potatoes had finished I did a variety of jobs for Footmans, if I was needed Mr. Footman would ring the night before and his wife would come and pick me up. In the small depot was a storage building for Spillers flour that was used by that company as a base for deliveries in S.W. Wales. I would load flour at Spillers in Avonmouth for the flour depot in Footman's yard, the loads were about eighteen pallets and nice and low so dead easy to sheet. Sometimes I was on the tipper trailer moving grain around, which was a good easy job. I was still driving the mini-bus and helping the builder now and again, there was nothing set in stone about these two jobs.

One day I was needed to load a trailer of animal feed potatoes from a farm near the coast in Pembrokeshire, the potatoes were coated with a purple dye to signify that they were animal feed only. It was a bit messy loading and I was alone in a field handballing the bags off farm trailers, I was glad when I had finished but not dis-pleased at all with the work. Mr Footman had told me where the farm I was deliver the potatoes to was located and said that I would have to approach the farm from a certain direction on a single track road. The reason being that it was impossible to turn around at the farm. I thought that it was a long way around so I went my own way, managing to turn around between two farm buildings, the farmer said it was the first time it had been done. With about six of us unloading it did not take long and as is the way in the countryside, I was invited into the farmhouse for a meal, and very nice it was to.

Charles Footman made Donald Malcolm seem like an angel, he had a terrific temper and it was always do as I say or else. Other times he was friendly and chatty so on the whole he was not a bad boss really. The entrance to his yard was on the side of the A485 at Alltwalis and approaching from the south it was on the right and easy to enter, coming from the north he said everyone had to pass the yard and turn around to approach from the south. I came from the north one day and thought sod it, I can get in without turning, no problem. There was no traffic around so I swung out to my right and then turned left towards the yard entrance.

The back of the trailer was practically in the yard and there was a couple of inches clearance from the nearside gate-post when Mr. Footman charged out of the house waving his arms and looking like thunder. I was in the yard but he made me reverse out onto the road and go and turn round as per his standing orders, he could be a bit hard to handle when he did things like that, still it was fun to do a bit of baiting.

Things fell apart after about eighteen months in Wales when Liz and I split up, I think she had decided that living in Wales was not for her. We both returned to Preston and eventually got back together, we even started a small business in Preston and for a few years everything seemed fine but it was not to be long lasting. We split up again and I walked away from the Preston business, Liz took it over and it is still going today, a very big concern nowadays, something I could never have built up. I did a couple of local van driving jobs for a few months and after meeting my present wife Val I asked her to come back to Wales with me. We were very lucky in renting a small cottage set in half an acre in the village of St. Brides in Pembrokeshire. It was a wonderful place not another house to be seen and only half a mile from the coast and St. Brides Bay. I had let my H.G.V. licence lapse and was deeply shocked when I failed the medical, the main reason for the failure being my old head injury. (As I am writing this I have received my letter from the hospital for my bi-annual scan). This put the cat amongst the pigeons but undaunted I went full circle and went back working on a farm. By this time I was in my fifties but in really good health so going on the farm was not a problem.

It was great walking to work across a couple of fields, I had never felt better about things for a good while. The farm was a very large arable farm, growing over seventy acres each of cauliflowers and potatoes. In addition some beef cattle and tack sheep were kept but the main use of the farm was for the crops. I arrived just at the time when most of the potatoes were to be planted. All the seed potatoes had been stored in low, open wooden crates stacked twelve foot high in the sheds. There were thousands of the crates in long lines in the sheds, this was to allow the potatoes to chit or grow some root on them, my first job on the farm was to stand on a pallet on the large agricultural fork-truck and work my way down the stacks loading the pallets. They were then put on trailers and taken to the fields. The driver, a local man called Eric watched my every move and because of his driving I never had to reach up or down and over-reach to lift any crate. It was hard graft but with Eric on the fork-truck a cracking rhythm was established that was hardly ever broken. We worked away at this for a couple of weeks until we had emptied the sheds. I had stacked a few hundred tons of potatoes, thousands of crates, every single one, and I never ever felt better, with not a twinge from my back.

After the potatoes I did a fair bit of tractor driving in the fields driving a big John Deere tractor that even had a radio, a far cry from the old Fordson Major I had driven nearly forty years before. Next to come was the cauliflowers, all seventy acres of them, and they were all destined for Tesco supermarkets. About seven or eight women from the Pembroke and Milford area did the chopping in the fields dressed in yellow oil-skins. Some of them were in their sixties and had done this work for years. I tried my hand at chopping but as Tescos were particular and wanted a clean cut right at the base of the cauliflower my efforts were not very good. I was chopping and leaving too much stalk on or slicing the cauliflower itself and this was no good. I went on the trailer stacking the full crates, it was out of any bad weather as the trailer was covered and in the fields next to the sea the views were fantastic. It took weeks and weeks to harvest all the cauliflowers, it felt like there was millions of them. As the months past it was time for the potato harvest. A large covered harvester was used for this but it still required half a dozen women on the machine to pick any stones off the conveyer belts. Some parts of the fields were very stony and the tractor had to tow the machine very slowly as the women could not keep up. On sloping fields two tractors had to be used to pull the harvester creating huge ruts in the soil as they climbed the hill. In the winter months the cycle of the potatoes went on with all the crates being filled with seed potatoes and stacked in lines in the chitting sheds. This was a lot harder work than emptying the sheds but I managed along with some help from the others. I used to get some stick from the Welsh because I was English, mainly "Shut the door when you leave" or "when are you going home" but it was all in fun and I enjoyed the banter.

Our cottage was a wilderness when we took it over and I had spent hundreds of hours in the gardens. I had dug over very large area and planted grass seed to make a huge lawn with curvy flower beds in some areas. I grew all my own bedding plants in a homemade greenhouse and had planted some vegetables in another area. Val and I had made a long picket fence out of old pallets from the farm. Once painted and in place around the front garden it looked great, it also kept stray sheep out of the garden.

It all ended after over two years when the owner of the cottage came and told us that he wanted to sell the cottage. The asking price was way beyond me and even the villagers were upset at the price as it meant locals could not afford it either. Prices for cottages were on the rise because of the demand for second or holiday homes. We looked around for something else to rent but everything was too expensive for the money I was earning. The day came when the cottage was sold to a retired university lecturer from the Midlands. That was that, I was bitterly disappointed but could not compromise on a lesser property so we walked away from Wales.

CHAPTER SIX
STILL DRIVING

My daughter Sally who is a school teacher lives with her policeman husband and their three children in Cirencester, my son David who after serving ten years in the Royal Marines was now also a policeman and lives in Cheltenham with his Policewoman wife. They both wanted us to go and live in Gloucestershire, it was a lot more expensive area to live in but that's where we decided to go. We found a small cottage to rent in the village of Kemble just south of Cirencester. With the larger rent I needed a decent job pretty quickly, with no H.G.V. licence I would have to set my sights lower, but not as low as some of the jobs I saw in the Job Centre. Without too much trouble I was offered a job with a company called Logistic Support Services who were based in one of the large WW2 aircraft hangers on Kemble airfield. The job was driving a MAN seven and a half ton box van delivering pallets that arrived overnight from the Pallex hub in the midlands. The area covered was most of Gloucestershire and all of Wiltshire, with a lot of the drops in the main towns in the two counties, the vans had tail lifts and I couldn't see any problems. The boss explained that I would be expected to do at least a sixty hour week, the extra hours to be used delivering parts from the hanger storage area to the Dyson factory in Malmesbury. This was good news and I calculated that when Val got a job we would be not too badly off. L.S.S had the two MAN box vans, three Leyland Daf artics and an old Seddon Atkinson that was used for Pallex night work. The hanger was huge and it was possible to imagine it full of Spitfires in the war, at a couple of places on the airfield could be seen where the Spitfires shot any unused ammunition into a bunker before the guns were serviced and then tested afterwards. The company had Irish links as they also collected groupage traffic for over the water. My first couple of weeks were really a matter of finding where the drops were, but as many were repeated during the week it got a lot easier. We also had collections to do in the afternoons including two trips every day to Bourton-on-the-Water to collect palleted stone fireplaces from a stone quarry. On the whole the boss got his pound of flesh out of the drivers but the work was easy enough once the drops were sorted.

Val got a job in House of Fraser in Cirencester so we were well sorted for jobs and money. We saw a lot of my family and it was good to see my grandchildren who I not seen much of in the past few years. I was doing up to sixty five hours a week mainly on the Pallex and Dyson work but occasionally I went into London collecting groupage to stuff artic box vans at Kemble. I had been doing this for around eighteen months when I had another accident. I was delivering a pallet of stone cladding to a pub being restored in Wotton-under-Edge, I could tell by the bending of the tail-lift that the pallet was well past the maximum one ton limit that Pallex allowed, I reckoned it was near to double that. The pallet had to go round the back of the pub over loose chippings. I was walking backwards and pulling and the builders were pushing from behind, the next thing I knew I fallen on my back and the two small wheels on the pallet truck were on top of my foot. I remember shouting for them to get it off, they pulled it back off my foot but I knew it was not good. The builders sat me on a wall and I took my boot off, the boots had steel toe-caps but the damage was on the top of my foot. An ambulance was called and it hurt like hell while I was waiting, it duly arrived and I was taken to Frenchays hospital in Bristol. Two bones on the top of the foot were broken and the outside of the foot was gashed open. They nurses cleaned me up and a cast was put on my foot and halfway up my shin. The boss's wife came to collect me and told me not to worry as I would still get basic pay which was good to know. That evening I was in a lot of pain and went to Cirencester hospital where they took the cast off. Val nearly fainted when she saw my foot, it was not a pretty sight but after being cleaned up again they put a soft cast on the foot and it was a lot better from then on.

A couple of days later the boss came round and asked was I okay to work in the office for a few weeks, I didn't really want to but felt as he was paying me a basic wage I couldn't refuse. Really I should have rested my foot and kept it raised so hobbling around the office on crutches or with my feet under a desk did the healing process no good at all. The boss asked me a few times if I was going to claim compensation, I should have said yes, but told him no I wasn't. After about ten weeks I was told I could return to normal duties but to be careful. The first day back I jumped off the back of a trailer without thinking and that really hurt.

After about two years anyone could see things were not going well at L.S.S, work was drying up and the pallets were down by half. I asked the boss about the lost work and he just said it was his problem and nothing to do with me. Two days before Christmas he made us all redundant, hardly leaving us enough time to get to the Job Centre before the holidays. I made my mind up there and then I was going to get compensation for my accident. Moving on three years from that day I got £4500, it would have been more but it was determined that I was 50% at fault for moving a knowingly overloaded pallet.

After that Christmas I dropped really lucky and got another job by the second week of January. This time I was to do nation-wide deliveries of expensive handmade beds and bedroom furniture with a new Renault Master van, I was to become a white van man. The job was salaried at around £15000 which was pretty good for driving a van. The company had a small factory employing around a dozen workers, the sleigh beds they made cost up to £ 2500 and even a small chest of drawers was around £1000. The deliveries where to John Lewis warehouses and furniture shops all over England and up to Glasgow in Scotland. The van was fast and it needed to be, one job was from Cirencester into the Lake District with two furniture shop deliveries, then up to John Lewis in Glasgow, across to John Lewis in Edinburgh finishing up at John Lewis in Newcastle, and all in one day. With no Cumbria drops I used to be waiting outside the John Lewis warehouse in Glasgow at 8-30 am on the first day. I stayed in the Newcastle airport motel that night and had a steady drive back to Cirencester the next day. Not all days where as bad as that, the deliveries to London and around the M 25 were easy. Penzance and Cornwall was a bit of a slog, I was usually in Penzance by 8am. Kent was difficult as the deliveries also took in towns around the Wash. Cambridgeshire and Norfolk were one delivery area and it was quite a few miles on that longish run. One particular day I did Cirencester to Glasgow and return in one go with an urgent delivery, on the return journey when I was around the Stoke area I got my second wind and did not feel at all tired. I drove the van for the next three years until Val said she wanted to move back to Lytham as she was missing her family. I had to agree to her request, she had been away from them for a few years and had really done what I had wanted most of the time. As I was approaching 60 years old the problem of how to earn a living was on my mind, not many firms would take a 60 year old, in a supermarket maybe but not much else. I had been told by a few parcels carriers in Gloucestershire that it was a younger man's job, even the boss in my present job had cheekily said was I up to doing the job, and asked about my health.

I therefore decided to try to get a hackney license to drive a taxi in Lytham St. Annes, I got the forms by post and booked a medical. I was not sure how it would go but strangely enough I passed it. There didn't seem to be continuity between different doctors, it was too late now but maybe a lesser doctor not up on the law would have passed me to get my H.G.V. licence back. I remember the doctor who failed me showing me all the all the medical jargon that he had to consult to reach a decision. We moved back to Lytham, rented a nice quiet bungalow, and started again. We both got jobs right away, Val was taken on at a large lighting, card and gift shop in Lytham a job she likes and is still there today. I was taken on at Whitesides taxis in St. Annes, a big long established company that was a cut above the usual taxi firms. All the drivers had to wear black trousers, black shoes, blue shirts and a company tie. All the fleet was made up of white cars some being company cars and others owner drivers, most of the drivers being close to my age or older. The white cars were inspected every week and had to be valeted before the inspection. We were required to get out of the car and open and close the doors for female passengers, and to assist all elderly customers with shopping and other bags. It was all a good thing really, making the service one of the best in the Fylde. It got up the noses of the Blackpool taxi drivers, most of who were decidedly scruffy. We did a lot of work in Blackpool, not a place I like, but needs must as they say. For a couple of years I was doing six days a week and eleven or twelve hours a day. The money was not bad if you were prepared to work at it. It was no good sitting on a rank waiting for work to come to you, it had to be looked for. Some, but not all drivers knew where certain jobs were due and on what days, the whole coast was divided into plots and if you were the first on that particular plot you got the job. The screen in the taxi also showed where and when pre-booked jobs were due. If no other cars were on that plot it was a quick dash to be the first there, it didn't always work out but it was worth a try. Train station jobs were the best, Blackpool North from St.Annes was over ten pounds, and Preston station was around twenty pounds. A call to the office from Preston and there was the possibility of a return fare which was an ideal situation. I believe it has all changed now, mainly because there are just too many taxis. The other drivers were a real cross section of previous occupations, ex lorry drivers, retired policemen, school teachers, tradesmen, ex-servicemen, there was even a retired bank manager.

I drove the taxi until just before I was sixty four when I had a heart scare. I had a stent fitted in the Cardiac Centre in Blackpool, a few months later I was back at the Cardiac Centre again and it was getting a bit worrying. My medical for the taxi licence was done in Cirencester and my doctor in Lytham was shocked that I passed the medical, he said he would not have passed me. My doctor now told me that my days of driving a taxi were over and he would not pass me as fit, retirement was upon me. I had planned to work on until nearer seventy but now accepted that it was now over.

I had worked for fifty years, most of it doing hours that were near double the normal forty hour week, it never bothered me, I never felt unfit or tired out, it was just something that anyone can get used to and became a way of life.

Accidents apart I would do most of it again especially the docks, N.I.T. and of course W.H. Malcolms. I could not do it in the present time though, it was only 50 years, not long in the scale of things but so much has changed in that fifty years, never to return.

I now spend my time looking after Val who has a few years to go before she retires, we go camping with the family and have weekends away. I enjoy all football and make large wooden sailing ships, I have a large collection of military books, a subject I am passionate about. My collection of ship models and photos is growing all the time so all in all I have enough to keep me occupied. Val and I have just had a week in Scotland, a country I love, a move there is in our minds, why break the habits of a lifetime.

THE END

PHOTO COURTESY OF GYLES CARPENTER

Printed in Great Britain
by Amazon